Joy That Renews

Steve Akerson

Joy That Renews

A devotional from Psalms
to refresh your life every day

Steve Akerson

RIVER BIRCH PRESS

Daphne, Alabama

Note to Readers:

Free Study Guide Available

The author has prepared a *Joy That Renews Study Guide* to help readers discover the depth of what these verses have to say. Whether a reader is a small group leader or is using this guide for their own personal study, this guide will help release more joy as you look into Psalms. Please go to joythatrenews.com, click on Study Guide, complete the form, and the Study Guide will be mailed to you free of charge.

ISBN 978-1-951561-78-9 (print)
ISBN 978-1-951561-79-6 (e-book)

For Worldwide Distribution
Printed in the U.S.A.

River Birch Press
P.O. Box 868, Daphne, AL 36526

Contents

Introduction

Are you hungry to experience more lasting joy in your life? As you read these verses, you will feel joy pulsing through both the trials and victories written about in Psalms. Do you wonder if God really loves you? His steadfast love will jump off these pages and be very real to you.

Does the thought of God's goodness leave you wondering how it applies to you? You will see David and Moses (people who are very much like you) agonize about their difficulties, but always find themselves pointing back to and relying on God's amazing goodness to live a life of victory and purpose.

Do you feel like you are stuck in a bad place? You will feel wonder in the release God gives you—even if you put yourself in the bad place to begin with. You will feel power over the past that has been plaguing you. God will lift you out of your prison and put you in a sweet place where you will be free from shame and guilt. You will be moved (perhaps to tears as I have been) and worship the Lord as you realize the greatness of your freedom.

This book came to be when I asked God to show me one specific verse out of each chapter of Psalms to study. Right away I started hearing God speaking to me in very personal ways. I felt amazingly energized each day to find anew God's joy, peace and love.

I entered into each day with a great sense of expectation and fresh excitement to see what the Lord had for me that day. He very quickly made one verse in each chapter stand out—He caught my attention and fired my imagination with these individual verses. The results in my life were fantastic and I fell more in love with Jesus every day.

This same sense of adventure is waiting for you. As you think about each verse you will have the opportunity to hear Jesus talk with you about it. Your thoughts will be engaged as you understand the incredible gifts he wants to give you—maybe most importantly the gift of total acceptance. You'll see that God doesn't limit his love or joy for you; in fact, his desire is to pour them all over you every day—no matter what is happening to you that day.

You will see how these verses, written thousands of years ago are precisely relevant to you today. The feelings they had back when they were writing are the same ones you feel each day. In many ways their situations are similar to yours. And the solutions they found and write about are effective, easy to understand and powerful.

I invite you into this adventure of experiencing the lavish love and ongoing joy God has for you. I'd encourage you to take your time pondering each verse and write down your thoughts in the bottom margin of each page—that practice will help you dive into each verse and get out of it all that God has for you. Welcome to a fantastic journey—you will be amazed at God.

One important decision to make when you are writing a devotional is what translation of the Bible you are going to use. I selected *The Passion Translation*. I was blessed to be introduced to this version by a leader in my church. I started reading it and fell in love with it. I believe it does a great job of putting you in the situation. The language is compelling and inspiring. I heard the Lord speaking through the words and was energized by the texts. I recommend checking it out.

Themes from the Psalms

Psalms is a unique and wonderful book in the Bible. It's like reading 150 different short stories—stories about people experiencing life in all its many flavors. There are chapters and verses that highlight great events and victories. And there are writings describing very difficult circumstances and failings. You will feel the ups and downs as you consider what theses verses mean for you.

In my preparation I noticed there are themes that tie these various stories and situations together. I think having an understanding of these themes will be helpful for your understanding the Psalms, and more importantly for being able to see yourself in them. These themes paint a picture of what I saw God saying through the Psalms. I know they will lift your spirit as you get ready to dive into these verses.

God's Goodness

We have a saying in our church that goes "God is good, all the time. All the time, God is good." I used to take that saying for granted. After reading in depth through the Psalms and writing about these verses I won't do that anymore. The richness, depth and intention of God's goodness changed my life.

God's goodness is part of his character. He treats you with goodness, kindness and understanding because his character is good, and only good. To the core of his very being, God is good. That impacts everything he has done and will do in the future. It gives you confidence that though the world sometimes doesn't seem to make sense, you can always count on the Lord to be good to you. No matter what you face, look at Jesus and see that he will bring you only good.

God's Steadfast Love and Faithfulness

These words are used in many of the verses you will read about in this devotional. They are outcomes of his goodness. The writers of the Psalms are very transparent about the dangers and disappointments they faced. And they are equally clear that through whatever is happening to them, they recognize God's steadfast love and faithfulness are present and active in their lives.

You will see how this truth touches the lives of the authors in amazing ways. They will be taken, sometimes abruptly, from despair to gladness as they recall God's love and call out to him for more. These characteristics of the Lord will be a solid foundation for you and provide you with hope even when things look bad. You will learn the value of knowing that Jesus' love is pure and nonending. It will change the reality of your life.

Living in Freedom

You are going to read lots of verses that talk about how the Lord will break the chains that bind you and keep you from living in freedom. The Lord values your freedom as much as anything else he wants to give to you. In fact, the Bible says: "For freedom Christ has set you free." Freedom is so important that he gives it to you for its own sake.

He knows that you will not be happy in your life if you are captured by sin and its addictions. He promises that his power and authority are more than enough to bring you freedom from whatever might be trying to keep you stuck. He wants you to be able to live like you've always wanted to, and to be who you've always wanted to be. He has the power to make these happen for you.

Joy and Praise

You are going to have your world rocked by how much joy these verses are going to bring you. You will feel your heart being filled with joy by God as you think about his goodness and love for you and then thank him for these powerful and life changing gifts. You will see that the joy you are given will be lasting and deep. It will help you overcome situations and difficulties that you face.

And you will learn how to become a joy-creator. Yes, you will be able to generate joy in your life and the lives of those around you. The fuel that generates joy is your worship and praise of the Lord. These verses will lead you into praise and you will see your heart creating joy and gladness in you. No matter what is going on in your life, you can quietly or out-loud worship Jesus, and he will bring a deep-seated and lasting joy to you.

Being Thankful

Closely related to joy are the many, many verses that talk about thanksgiving. There are going to be things that happen in your life that will bring you disappointment, hurt and sorrow. God's word consistently says to be thankful in, but not for these things. It doesn't make sense to be thankful for a diagnosis of cancer. But you can learn to be thankful to God even when you, or a loved one, gets that news.

Being thankful at all times is a sign that you are living in freedom, that you refuse to be captive to the events of life. It also shows that you recognize that God is in control, not you. Being thankful even in the face of bad news will release you from the dread of the news and put you on solid ground to deal with the situations with a clear mind. And a thankful mindset is one of the means by which God delivers goodness into your life

Hearing God's Voice

David and the other writers of the Psalms clearly heard God speaking to them. You can read God speaking to you in every verse you read. Its a release when you hear God—it shows you that he is always wanting to interact with you. He longs to hear your voice, and also for you to hear his. Remember as you read the verses that they are God's words to you.

And as you get more and more used to asking God about his written words, you will learn that you can ask him questions and that he will answer you. And you will be eager to hear from him. Practice this—open your hands and give God something that you don't want—maybe anger or fear. Then when you have given that to the Lord, ask him what he wants to give you in return. You will learn to recognize his voice in your mind and heart, and you will be so encouraged. He will respond with only good and positive things for your life; his words will give you courage, peace and joy. You will be prepared to move into whatever is happening with hope and confidence.

1

River of Life

Seek the water of God's nourishment; soak in it every day.

He will be standing like a flourishing tree planted by God's design, deeply rooted by the brook of bliss, bearing fruit in every season of his life. He is never dry, never fainting, ever blessed, ever prosperous (Psalm 1:3).

Imagine yourself as this tree, growing in a specific place that has been selected by your King—a place that is purposefully located to be best for you. That's exactly what the Lord does. Why? To make sure you are continually nourished by his brook of bliss, the stream the Lord uses to help you flourish in every area of your life.

This brook is everything God has designed for you and given to you, to help you be full of joy—that great combination of peace, contentment, hope, power, and love. God's brook will supply you all the time—in good seasons and bad. You will prosper and have enough to love and be loved. Your growth, like a tree, will be natural, coming from the brook. It will seep into every area of your life.

And when you find yourself in a desert place where you face hardships, sorrows or fears sink your roots deeper. In this digging, you will find the Lord's refreshing water.

———◆———

This urges me to always seek the water of God's written Word and the words he speaks to my heart. I love that he has a place of nourishment for me. The closer I live with Jesus, the more I will prosper, grow, and be fully alive.

2

The Joy of Humility

**Our God is awesome. It is wonderful to be
in humble presence before him.**

*Serve and worship the awe-inspiring God. Recognize his
greatness and bow before him, trembling with reverence in his
presence* (Psalm 2:11).

What's the most awe-inspiring thing you can think of? How
about a majestic mountain range, or a new baby? However great
those gifts are, God is infinitely more awesome.

It's just incredible that you get to serve and worship this astonishing God! He welcomes you at his table and is eager to hear your
prayers and your singing in worship (even if you can't sing well).
He longs for you to be deeply involved in who he is—God's level
of desire for you is almost beyond thought.

The truth that the Lord is so much bigger than you are is comforting. He can handle the big things that happen in your life and
in the world around you. Knowing that Jesus has his eyes on you
and will bring you freedom in all circumstances creates hope and
peace in your life.

Your world is full of people who are also hungry for the Lord's
love. You can bring them encouragement, hope, joy, and peace.
Pour out words of gladness over them—you both will love it.

It is so peaceful to place myself under God, to be humble before him, knowing that he is far greater than I am and way more
powerful than my problems. I've learned that he can and does
make himself clear to me even in my bad times. This makes me
want to bow before him and give him my obedience, my heart, and
all my concerns.

3

Shame Destroyed

With Jesus, you will live without shame.

But in the depths of my heart I truly know that you, Yahweh, have become my Shield; You take me and surround me with yourself. Your glory covers me continually. You lift high my head when I bow low in shame (Psalm 3:3).

Being trapped in shame will ruin your life. It doesn't have to be so; you can be free. Don't hang onto your sin and guilt. Confess your sins; repent right away. Using the authority of Jesus, command the enemy of shame to leave your life. Practicing these steps will break the back of shame in your life. You will live in security instead of anxiety.

Life teaches that you can't be your own protector. With Jesus shielding you from your foes, you don't have to worry about your past. Keep your focus on Jesus, he will take care of you. Believers, learn to love the picture of Jesus surrounding you with his glory—put that in your imagination and rest in it.

You will grow to live with your head lifted high. Jesus has removed your shame; he has shredded your guilt and demolished your fears and replaced them all with the joy of living in freedom from anything in your past.

Let God be your glory; let him take away the shame of your past and the fear of the future. He will change your life.

—————

Learning the value of confessing and repenting from my sins and of using my spiritual authority to command God's enemies to leave me has saved my life. Knowing that Jesus has completely destroyed my sin and shame fills me with hope.

4

Contented Sheep

You will live in safety and with a peaceful heart and mind.

Now, because of you, Lord, I will lie down in peace and sleep comes at once, for no matter what happens, I will live unafraid! (Psalm 4:8).

If you have kids or grandchildren, your heart has melted watching them sleep. They are amazingly still and peaceful! The ability to relax and sleep like that is precious. The world is so full of anxiety and worry, people are desperately trying to figure out how to get that much peace. You know it can only be found in Jesus.

As a believer, you can live—each and every day—in peace, comfort, and contentment. You can live this way even when things seem to be tumbling around you, and your hopes are not realized. Jesus has paid the price for you to live in peace, no matter what you face. That, fellow believers, is beyond anything the world could ever give you.

Sleep can sometimes be hard. Fix your mind on the fact that your safety has been bought by Jesus. Remind yourself that your security doesn't come from your job, your family, or your bank account. Nobody but Jesus can bless you in such a powerful, life-changing way. The Lord's gifts are steady and constant. You will live without any fears; they fall apart in the lap of Jesus.

———◆———

I won't let circumstances—even when they are breaking my heart—steal my joy, my rest, or my contentment. The more I learn to lean into Jesus and climb up in his lap and listen to his heartbeat, and the more I worship him, the more I have the kind of peace that surpasses anything I could imagine.

5

Listen Up

God is eager to hear your voice, and he will speak to you.

At each and every sunrise you will hear my voice as I prepare my sacrifice of prayer to you. Every morning I lay out the pieces of my life on the alter and wait for your fire to fall upon my heart (Psalm 5:3).

When your phone rings and it's your son or daughter on the other end, your face immediately breaks out in a big smile as you hear good news from them. That's what the voice of the Lord is like—it restores and renews your hope and joy. Just like talking, prayer is a two-way conversation. As you talk to the Lord, take time to sit still and listen for his voice too.

Your Father knows it isn't always easy to pray. Time, work, and hassles all can get in the way. David was far from perfect, but one thing he did great was that he prayed to his King every day. Some days, just like you, all he had were "the pieces" of his life.

Jesus knows that and is eager to bring comfort and hope to you. Worship him quietly and out loud. And don't hurry, let yourself settle down before the Lord. He will bring his fire to your heart and renew your life every day.

A Bible teacher I like a lot says that "God has a lot more talk than I have listen." I'm finding that to be so true. How do I know when God has spoken to me? He only speaks in love. Everything he says to me will be good for me and others. I won't get any type of condemnation from him—only love.

6

Dig Deep

Your Father will always show you mercy and grace.

Please deal gently with me, Yahweh; show me mercy, for I'm sick and frail. I'm fading away with weakness. Heal me, for I'm falling apart (Psalm 6:2).

What if you get a call from one of your kids, and it's bad, even shattering news? This is the nitty-gritty of life. What can you do when even the worst happens? Everyone is in this place at one time or another; nobody is immune. In these times, David has some good practices to follow:

Call out to the Lord, asking for his mercy and grace. Be honest with him about how you feel. Continue to call out to him. Wait to hear from him, believing by faith that he hears you and will answer you, especially when your pain is great.

There are going to be times when his mercy and grace seem far off. In those times you will need to dig deeper to find his brook of nourishment. Don't give in to despair or unbelief. Practice believing even when all you feel is pain. God will come through for you in the way that is best for your life.

Whatever your pain is, claim by faith that God's steadfast love and mercy are surrounding you right now. Hang in there and take time to wait until you hear God's voice. It will come.

———◆———

I know my Father knows my pains and sorrows and that he will always be merciful and gracious with me. I will remind myself of that, run to him, and make him my refuge where I will live in safety.

7

Plant Thankfulness, Reap Joy

Practicing thankfulness and praise will grow joy in your life.

But I will give all my thanks to you, Lord, for you make every-thing right in the end. I will sing my highest praise to the God of the Highest Place! (Psalm 7:17)

Have you ever had anyone respond to your word of thanks with a grouchy look and a sharp word? Instead, you are most likely going to create a positive moment for both of you. The value of living with a thankful attitude is beyond measure.

- Being thankful will help you overcome the darkness you see around you every day.
- It will help you overcome other not-so-good attitudes that may crop up, such as anger, fear, judgment. These things are life-destroyers; thankfulness is a life-giver.
- It will help take your eyes off temporary problems you face and keep them on Jesus and your Father, where blessings, mercy, grace, and peace flow.
- It will encourage you and everyone around you. Being thankful will change your life.

This verse points out the relationship between thankfulness and God's gift of making things right—his righteousness. That is very uplifting because God's righteousness is eternal, and it covers everything. As you practice giving thanks to the Lord, you will gain more freedom to be who you really want to be. And thankfulness will also lead to praising God, which will lift your heart and produce contentment and joy.

The combination of thankfulness and the resulting content-ment is very powerful for me. I want to breathe deeply in it and practice it so it surrounds me, which will make me happier, more joyful, and filled with peace.

8

Better than the Best

Our Lord is THE Lord. He seeks us out to lavish his love and care on us.

Lord, your name is so great and powerful! People everywhere see your splendor. Your glorious majesty streams from the heavens, filling the earth with the fame of your name! (Psalm 8:1)

When I was growing up, I always wanted my baseball glove to say "Genuine Leather" on it. Coca Cola® brags about being the "real thing." We all want the authentic antique, not the imitation.

Have you thought how blessed you are to have *the* Lord, be *your* Lord? There is great hope and assurance in that. You can know that your faith is well-placed, and the Creator of the entire universe is on your side. He is forever for you.

God's majesty sets him apart, above everything and everyone. He is awesome and overwhelming. He shows his magnificence in the big majestic things he created like the stars and beauty around you, as well as in the small, intimate things he created such as newborn babies. Your Lord is the God of the huge and the tiny—nothing escapes him!

Worship and praise this transcendent King who knows the cries of babies. How great and majestic is a God like that! It shows me that the world is *not* spinning out of control; instead, he brings peace to the jumble we sometimes feel.

<hr />

God comforts me with his character and with the certain knowledge that he cares about every aspect of my life. Somehow in his majesty over all of creation, he still focuses like a laser on my life. Thank you, Lord, that your care and your love search me out.

9

God's Eagerness

**God's mercy is always flowing on and in you,
turn to Him to experience it all.**

*May everyone who knows your mercy keep putting their trust
in you, for they can count on you for help no matter what. O
Lord, you will never, no never, neglect those who come to you*
(Psalm 9:10).

No situation you face, whether good or bad, is too much for
the Lord. He is more than able and ever willing to take care of you,
no matter what! His mercy—when we don't get what we do deserve—coupled with his grace—when we do get what we don't deserve—are overwhelming and bring a settled peace to your life and
outlook.

Trust is tough to come by in today's world. It is an act of faith
when you choose to trust. Your trust is not blind; it is based on the
Lord's character and actions. For thousands of years God has been
healing, rescuing, and setting people free.

Trust is always rewarded by God, especially when trusting is
the hardest, like in the heartbreak of a child's death, the loss of a
job, or the love of your life. Trust, in those times, means you have
purposefully chosen to believe in the Lord's steadfast love and
faithfulness. Speak your faith and trust out loud, soak in the
thought of it, especially if you feel far from it.

God's mercy and his grace are full of his authority. When I
need it most, I turn to him and seek them. I trust that he is eager
to hear me. He considers me fully worthy of his love.

10

Don't Shrink Back

Your Father sees your problems. With him you will walk in increasing power.

Lord, you know and understand all the hopes of the humble and will hear their cries and comfort their hearts, helping them all! (Psalm 10:17)

Does it seem like sometimes the enemy is running rampant, and everything is upside down—evil behavior is celebrated, and those of faith are ridiculed, pushed aside, and deemed not relevant. This verse promises you that God hears the needs, cries, and requests of his people.

To some degree and at various times, we are all under attack. A life of ease is never promised in the Bible. But you are assured that your Father does hear you, and you are not alone. That doesn't mean that your afflictions will somehow be removed from you.

Rather than a trouble-free life, God promises that you will be given the strength, wisdom, and grace to overcome your problems. Jesus, the King of the universe, will be actively involved in helping you through them.

Bring your desires and pains to the Lord, especially when you are in the midst of your biggest problems. That is not the time to shrink back but rather jump in closer to Jesus. He loves to hear you and make hope come alive for you.

No matter what's going on in my life, I rejoice that God sees and hears me. He will continue to listen and talk to me, strengthen me, and help me walk in more and more hope and power. His grace will continually create newness in me.

11

God's Total Rightness

Our God is righteous in all he is and does.

But remember this: The righteous Lord loves what is right and just, and every godly one will come into his presence and gaze upon his face! (Psalm 11:7)

The Lord is righteous. Totally. Completely. There is no hint of evil in him, which can be a strong source of strength for your daily walk with Jesus. He is righteous in all that he does, but even more than that, righteousness is the very essence of his being. Be encouraged to fall more in love with him, worship him, and raise your hands in praising him. It will make your life better.

The Lord is also building his character in you. As you get closer to Jesus, you can expect your life to become more righteous as well. Ask God for more of that character—he will love to hear and answer that prayer. As your behavior grows more to reflect Jesus, you will experience more peace in your life. You, and others around you, will see your inner character grow.

Remember the Lord is actively at work in you, transforming you to be more like him. Out of his great love for you, he is remaking you. And never forget that he calls you one of his godly ones.

———◆———

For me, this is almost more than I can take in. I have a new character, and it is getting renewed every day. I praise you, Jesus, for giving me such a great gift! I do gaze into Jesus' face with amazement.

12

Words of Life

The Lord will give you clear, trustworthy words to live by.

For every word God speaks is sure and every promise pure. His truth is tested, found to be flawless, and ever faithful. It's as pure as silver refined seven times in a crucible of clay (Psalm 12:6).

Who is the person in your life that you trust the most? Who lifts you up and speaks truth into you? Whose words make your heart glad? In addition to that person, you also have Jesus, whose advice will be absolutely true and perfect for every circumstance you face. What great comfort in knowing you can trust every word that God speaks to you! There are so many benefits to his trustworthy advice.

- His words have been tested for thousands of years. They have been put through the fire, and there is no impurity in them. His words will work in your life!
- His words are untainted; there is no selfishness in them. You can trust them to be good for you.
- You can count on the fact that everything God tells you, everything he asks of you, is for your benefit.
- There is no doubt in his words. No maybes.
- His words will bring your more joy.
- His words will help you make better decisions. They will never lead you down a path that is bad for you or others.
- His words are full of life and hope. They will lift up your soul.

God is my father or Abba (which means daddy or papa). As he is completely trustworthy, so are his words. I love learning to listen and hear his voice. I know he is keenly interested in talking to me and blessing me with his words.

13

You Choose

**Your life will be better as you focus on God's
tender care, not your problems.**

*Lord, I have always trusted in your kindness, so answer me. I
will yet celebrate with passion and joy when your salvation lifts
me up* (Psalm 13:5).

At this point, David was facing big problems. But he was also
learning that focusing on God's kindness brought him joy, even
when he saw no signs that pointed that way. He remembered that
God had been kind to him before, and he asks for more.

Life is really about what you choose to believe and focus on.
You can choose to believe that you are on your own, that God
doesn't hear you or care about you, which will lead to despair. *Or*
you can choose to believe his words and that his love is surrounding you, even in bad times. You can believe he is trustworthy,
which will lead to joy.

Take a step towards God—even if it is a tiny little step. Thank
him that he is kindness. Trust him just a little more; open your
heart to his love. These small steps will make a big difference in
your life. You will go from having a life filled with worry to one of
thankfulness and joy. You will feel your soul being lifted up—that's
God's love.

I have put myself in some big holes. In those times I have
found that focusing on Jesus, not the problem, leads to me seeing
more of God's love. I have come to realize that my King offers me
life—now and forever. That lifts me up and thrills my soul.

14

A Blessed Mulligan

Your life is being restored and made new; you will live with a glad heart.

How I wish that Israel's rescue would arise from the midst of Zion! When his people are restored, Jacob's joy will break forth and Israel will be glad! (Psalm 14:7)

In the game of golf, taking a mulligan means that you can forget all about the lousy shot you just made and start over and try again. That's what the Lord does for you. He has rescued you and restored your fortune (meaning your soul and spirit, not physical riches). You can rest and live with a peaceful heart and walk around with joy and gladness because of what Jesus has done for you. He is making you into a new and different person, and he's preparing a future for you that will be delightful.

Your rescue has arisen; you are being rejuvenated. Where you once thought you knew it all and were the center of it all, with humility you are now being refreshed every day into a life where your heart is filled with delight. Where you once disappointed yourself, you now live in freedom.

Your Lord has set you free from sins and addictions. He has crushed the life-killing shame and guilt that used to hang over your head. Every day you get to experience the freedom and joy that goes with walking with Jesus and being at peace with yourself.

I am redeemed. My life is a blessed mulligan. I live every day in the rescue Jesus has given me. I understand that he died to fill my life with gladness. I now experience more and more the life he has in mind for me—the life I want to live.

15

A Satisfied Life

Jesus has made you blameless.

They are passionate and wholehearted, always sincere and always speaking the truth—for their hearts are trustworthy (Psalm 15:2).

Who are these passionate and always sincere people? In another translation they are called blameless. But, in reality, who walks blamelessly? In the eyes of the Lord, *you* do! God has wiped away your sins and declared you blameless and righteous through the blood of Jesus. No matter your past, the Lord doesn't see your sins—he sees you as white as snow. Only Jesus and his obedience—to the point of death—could wipe away your sins and give you the power to live a life that satisfies you.

The Lord knows you will never live blamelessly, but you can live faithfully and passionately. Don't fall into the trap of just feeling bad when you sin—that's a recipe for losing intimacy with God. Instead, live faithfully by making it a practice to confess and repent (walk away) from your sins. God is glad when you confess and repent because it enables you to be closer to him. You will live with your head held high, with a lightness and sense of freedom because you will live like you've always wanted to live.

I don't always do the right thing; sometimes I sin. When I do, I will be quick to confess and repent. I will experience all the joy and freedom the Lord has for me. That means I will also see myself as free from sin, just like Jesus sees me.

16

Wise Choice

Live with joy on your path with Jesus.

The way you counsel and correct me makes me praise you more, for your whispers in the night give me wisdom, showing me what to do next (Psalm 16:7).

Remember the big decisions you have faced—where to go to school, what to major in, who should you marry, and so on. There are no easy answers to these questions, which can cause you to hesitate, and for some, it can even paralyze decision making.

It's a relief, and even more, a joy to know that the Lord really does give wisdom for these big choices. He promises to help you make these calls and to put you on a path that will cause you to praise him. That doesn't mean the path will be easy—you never know just where it will take you. The Lord allows you to see just a short way down the road because he wants you to live by faith and because he is gentle, knowing how much you can handle at any one time.

Learn to trust Jesus with the bumps and roadblocks you will face. His wisdom will be yours as you learn to listen for and hear his voice, which will bring you peace. While on your path, stay close to Jesus—only he has joy that sticks.

———•◆•———

God's wisdom, which leads to his forever pleasures, starts right now! I think of love for my wife, kids, and grandchildren, great friends, grace and mercy, and peace in my heart. How fantastic it is that the Lord releases these into my life every day! Thank you, Jesus.

17

The Twinkling Eye

God is your guard; he is always on your side.

Protect me from harm; keep an eye on me like you would a child reflected in the twinkling of your eye. Yes, hide me within the shelter of your embrace, under your outstretched wings (Psalm 17:8).

Whose eyes love you the best? Where do you see the joy in another person's eyes? A child, a spouse, a grandchild or grandparent are good bets. Those looks create tremendous joy, pride, and excitement.

It's the same with the Lord, whose eyes twinkle when he thinks of you. Imagine the love, hope, and pure acceptance reflected in that look. Another version says you are the apple of the Lord's eye. Both these are fantastic thoughts; they portray the truth and depth of God's love for you. He is always uplifting and gracious.

And on top of that, the Lord also shelters you in his embrace, which is exactly what we do for our children when they face problems. We want to give them the comfort that comes from a big hug. So, put aside any thought that your Father is angry or upset with you. Remember, he doesn't even remember your sins. He sees you as blameless—that's how great Jesus' gift to you is.

What a joy it is to be his child. He is so in love with you; there is always room for you in his embrace. Let that thought change your world.

I love that the Lord keeps me protected and continually showers me with his love. I love looking in his eyes, seeing them sparkle for me! Like a child, I envision being hugged by Jesus, basking in his look of love.

18

Hide and Found

Life can be very tough; take your refuge in the Lord.

What a God you are! Your path for me has been perfect! All your promises have proven true. What a secure shelter for all those who turn to hide themselves in you! (Psalm 18:30)

Your life has not been perfect. Like me, you have missed the mark many times. Sometimes this has been on purpose, other times by accident. You have been, at times, both a captive and a prisoner. This amazing promise says that from now on, when you follow his path, you can avoid the heartaches and disappointments that come from sin.

God wants nothing more than for you to be close to him. He is perfect in power and peace, in behavior and grace. He will never hurt you or cause you fear. God uses his perfect ways to make you better, not to manipulate or control you. He wants your life to be like his because he knows that is the best thing for you—it will create the most joy.

It's good that you need his shelter. He wants you to run into his refuge, to take comfort in him, even to hide in his protection and safety for a while, and to prepare for battles you may face. Run full speed into his refuge.

Life is sometimes very harsh, often because of my behavior. It won't always be pretty or neat. When I stay on his path and in his shelter, I am protected and nurtured. I can always trust him; he is holding me close.

19

Light-Hearted Living

Obeying God's commandments creates joy in your life.

His teachings make us joyful and radiate his light; his precepts are so pure! His commands, how they challenge us to keep close to his heart! The revelation-light of his word makes my spirit shine radiant (Psalm 19:8).

The Lord who created us has also created his ways and laws—that is the right and duty of the Creator. He is a Creator you can trust. He is true and does not change his mind, saying one thing one day and another the next. He is not selfish or short-sighted. His laws don't take away your joy; they enhance it. They are given out of his love, for your best. Obeying them creates joy!

God does everything he does for the purpose of lifting you up. All his commands are given to make you happier, more contented, more filled with joy and peace. Obeying his commands will produce a light heart in you and enable you to be ready to give and enjoy life.

God's greatest commandment is to love him with all your heart, soul, and mind, and to love others as yourself. As you do, you will see that the Lord's directions are pure and safe to follow. You will see your life being changed and experience greater joy and contentment.

———◆———

I realize more and more that God's words for me are not only true, but also they are the best for me. Following them makes my life better. My experience and my heart both agree this is true. Obeying the Lord brings me great hope and peace.

20

True Strength

Only the Lord can give you life-long security and happiness.

Some find their strength in their weapons and wisdom, but my miracle deliverance can never be won by men. Our boast is in the Lord our God, who makes us strong and gives us victory! (Psalm 20:7)

There are many things in life that will try to grab you. They will whisper to you that strength and security can be found in them; jobs, bank accounts and so on. These are all false hopes offering no real security. Stock markets go up and down. New and novel diseases cross the world, killing people everywhere. We are waking up again to the truth that physical things we put our hopes in will fail.

When you put more and more of your trust and faith in the Lord your perspective on "things" changes completely. You will realize this world isn't about stuff, it's about the Lord working in you to make your life richer in so many ways. Like living in freedom from sins and habits that drag you down. Like finding contentment and joy in your heart, not your back pocket. Like finding your future is full of direction, peace, purpose and contentment. These are the stuff of real life.

It is so easy for me to slip into trusting in things. I am a person who needs to be vigilant about putting the Lord first in everything, including my future. I have found that he is the only source to the strength I need to live with happiness and freedom in my heart.

21

Growing Joy

Praising God and worshiping him generates and releases joy in your life.

Your victory heaps blessing after blessing upon him. What joy and bliss he tastes, rejoicing before your face! (Psalm 21:6)

In this chapter, David is looking forward to his Redeemer, Jesus. What is striking is that these verses would also be true if written to and about you. God has promised to make you blessed (happy) forever with not just a little blessing but heaps of blessings. Can you imagine that—heaps of blessing! That can describe your life.

All of God's promises, just like this one, apply to you. They are all-inclusive for those who have put their faith in Jesus. He holds nothing back; there is no training period or time of probation. No matter your background, your personality, where you live, your race, your gender—none of those matter to the King. We are all equal and equally blessed!

How do you tap into this joy and bliss? One way is by rejoicing before God's face. When you worship, sing, praise, honor, and pray to your Lord, he responds by pouring out joy and bliss on you. What great gifts! This verse is one of many that shows God wants you to worship him not out of any need he has, but because it will make your life better. Worship will bring you joy!

God shows no favor. All his promises are mine to claim and by which to live. All he has to offer belongs to me. God is for me in everything. Being in God's presence is the best answer for my sadness, disappointment, or hurt. He is the best Friend you or I will ever have.

22

Handling Despair

**Your King is right next to you when you are hurting—
you are not alone.**

*For he has not despised my cries of deep despair. He's my first
responder to my sufferings, and he didn't look the other way
when I was in pain. He was there all the time, listening to the
song of the afflicted* (Psalm 22:24).

What do you do in times of despair? You probably reach out to
someone you love, who also loves you. You find comfort in that
deep connection, which also creates a sense of balance and hope.

People often cry out, "Where are you, God?" when they are
crushed by life. It's very human to feel like God doesn't really care
about the tough times you are going through. However, the truth is
that God never turns his back on you. He is your personal First
Responder! Remember that promise and grab ahold of it by faith
when life hurts.

The fact is that you won't live forever. Your life, or the lives of
those you love the most, may be shorter than you hope. You might
get sick, have financial troubles, or be betrayed.

As his beloved, grab ahold of your faith. Know that God
doesn't shrink back from you when you are heartbroken. Know that
he surely hears you when you cry out to him and he is by your side,
no matter what.

———

I can always bring my heartaches to Jesus and count on him to
hear me and respond. I am learning how to put my faith in the
Lord, not in my emotions, and to focus on the truth that he is right
next to me, always acting in ways that will bless me.

23

Chased by Goodness

God is chasing you down
to show you mercy and love.

So why would I fear the future? For your goodness and love pursue me all the days of my life. Then afterward, when my life is through, I'll return to your glorious presence to be forever with you! (Psalm 23:6)

Your first inclination at very good news is to run to your greatest love and tell them the news. They will celebrate with you, making your good news even better.

Similarly, your King can't wait to pour out good news and love on you. While you may face trouble and sorrows, your Lord and Father will bring you only goodness and mercy—and not just in heaven, but in all the days you have on earth.

Notice this verse doesn't say "good things" will pursue us every day, but that goodness and love will. God is pouring out his spirit of hope, kindness, joy, and forgiveness on you all the time. Not only that, he is seeking you out to give you those great gifts. Let yourself feel what that means to you!

You will always have a big choice in your life—either to focus on your problems or on God's goodness. That choice will make a tremendous difference in the quality of your life and on those around you. Learn to acknowledge, out loud, God's goodness and mercy whenever you see it. And practice being thankful—it will stir up joy in you.

———◆———

God has his eyes on me; he will bring me freedom; he will help me enjoy my life and have a positive outlook. Jesus is mercy; he has redeemed me and taken away my guilt. Praise Him!

24

An Order of Glory

The Lord will bring beauty and victory
to the battles in your life.

You ask, "Who is this King of Glory?" He is the Lord of Victory, armed and ready for battle, the Mighty One, the invincible commander of heaven's hosts! Yes, he is the King of Glory! (Psalm 24:10)

The King of Glory is the very God you worship. It is spectacular to see that God is in charge of all things that are glorious, beautiful, and great. When you are inspired by an awesome sight in nature, that is the King of Glory. When you see a brand-new baby and are filled with wonder, that is the King of Glory. When you see mercy being given to a person, that is the King of Glory!

He can order his things of glory (like honor, rightness, beauty) to show up where he wants them. If you want more of these in your life, get as close as you can to him, the King of Glory. He is able (strong and mighty) to do what he wants to accomplish in your life and demonstrate his love to you and through your life.

And he is ready and fully prepared for the issues you face. Do you face a job battle, an addiction battle, a battle against fear? The Lord is powerful over these and will bring you victory. Heaven's hosts are arrayed on your behalf.

———◆———

This is a strong and powerful verse. I choose to believe every word of it. I claim and rely on the King of Glory to bring glory to my life and make it meaningful and wonderful.

25

Let It Out

Be open and honest with the Lord; call on his mercy.

Sorrows fill my heart as I feel helpless, mistreated—I'm all alone and in misery! Come closer to me now, Lord, for I need your mercy (Psalm 25:16).

David was a man who used all his emotions, and he opened his heart to the Lord about them. Maybe it isn't easy for you to admit when you are feeling lonely and helpless. But it's dangerous to shove aside these deeper feelings, to try to live only in shallow waters, and just be just okay.

David's solution to his problem was to first admit what was going on with him and how it made him feel. And he didn't just think these things to himself—he wrote them down and got them out in the open. Finally, once he knew the truth of his situation, he looked to the Lord and called on him for mercy and help.

Don't hesitate to call out to Jesus when you are in great need. There is no embarrassment with Jesus. Turn your body, your mind, and your heart to him—put all your attention on him. Don't keep gazing at your problem—too much of that will drag you down. Jesus will fill your life with his mercy.

——◆——

I love the simple instructions in this verse—they make perfect sense to me. (1) Name my problem and emotions. (2) Say them out loud; get them out in the open. (3) Call on the Lord for his mercy and grace.(4) Believe I am receiving it even as I ask.

26

Move In

Fall in love with being close to Jesus, and with worshipping him.

Lord, I love your home, this place of dazzling glory, bathed in the splendor and light of your presence! (Psalm 26:8)

God's Word says that your body is the temple of the Holy Spirit. That means that you are the house where God's glory dwells. You don't need to go to a building or some special place; you are his house. God's glory dwells wherever he is welcomed, so make your house a great place for God's glory by continually inviting him to reign in your life.

You will be enriched as you more and more make the Lord a full-time resident in your house, not an occasional visitor. As you grow in seeking Jesus and engaging him in worship and prayer, your love for Jesus will grow, and you will love being who you are. That is joy—being made into the one you really want to be.

Let your time with Jesus be natural; don't feel pressure to learn anything. Feel the wonder of who Jesus is and what he is doing in your life. Talk to him, listen for his voice (he will talk with you, so practice listening) and thank him for what he gives you. Stillness before the Lord is a great gift to yourself.

━━◆◆◆━━

I count on the Lord to show me his glory and his beauty. That used to be an odd thought for me. But I am learning that Jesus is eager to show me himself. Sitting in wonder before him and his words raises my life up.

27

Surrender to Bravery

Soak in the goodness of the Lord, he will bring you through.

Here's what I've learned through it all: Don't give up; don't be impatient; be entwined as one with the Lord. Be brave and courageous, and never lose hope. Yes, keep on waiting—for he will never disappoint you! (Psalm 27:14)

David had faced death multiple times, and here he was about to be made king. His words of advice are timeless: do your best, don't give up, be brave, and keep on hoping. But most importantly, he said to be fully wrapped up in the Lord and to keep waiting to see God's goodness. He is the only one you can count on to get you through.

David also knew that other people will disappoint, and you know all too well that you will disappoint yourself. His final words of advice are so life-giving: to completely wrap yourself up with the Lord and to drink in the truth that he will never disappoint you.

The very bedrock of your life is to be totally given over to the Lord. As you give him more, you will live with growing confidence that your hope will make a difference. It is so wonderful to be assured that Jesus will never disappoint you. God doesn't hide his goodness; you will see it and experience how good the Father is to you each and every day.

There is great joy in surrender to Jesus. The more I live with and for him, the more of myself I let him have, which makes it easier for me to see God's goodness. All this leads to my life being increased.

28

Just a Little Faith

Trusting in the Lord produces great joy and thanksgiving.

You are my strength and my shield from every danger. When I fully trust in you, help is on the way. I jump for joy and burst forth with ecstatic, passionate praise! I will sing songs of what you mean to me! (Psalm 28:7)

David turns danger on its head, going from facing incredible trouble to being overcome with joy and exuberant praise. How does that kind of thing happen? It's simple but not easy. Turn your eyes to Jesus, proclaim him as your shield, put your trust fully in him, and praise his name and character. This is not always easy because faith is difficult at times. Ask the Lord every day to increase your faith and trust.

God's strength will help you move ahead into new things and new challenges. You don't need to fear the unknown. His shield protects you in your battles and is your defense against whatever seeks to cause you harm.

It doesn't take superhuman faith to live in this way. Faith as small as a mustard seed will unleash God's power and authority in your life. Taking even tiny little steps of faith will inspire you to do the same at your next challenge. Your joy will grow!

———◆———

When I take my mind off myself and put even just a little faith in Jesus, I am covered as I face new situations. When I dive into worship, my faith grows, as does my joy. I will keep on telling Jesus who he is in my life.

29

Worshipper Overboard

**You will rest in the beauty and
awesomeness of God's holiness.**

*Be in awe before his majesty. Be in awe before such power and
might! Come worship wonderful Yahweh, arrayed in all his
splendor, bowing in worship as he appears in the beauty of holiness. Give him the honor due his name* (Psalm 29:2).

The Lord is due all the glory you can possibly give him.
Worship him with the same fervor as you love your spouse or chil-
dren. Go overboard! He is mighty, the King of all, the Lord of all.
He is your homecoming, where your heart longs to be, the
Comfort of all the ages.

The Lord loves this kind of all-out worship. It honors him.
But equally true, this kind of worship is like a life-saving medicine
for you. It will take you from just hanging on to being fully alive.
As you get more comfortable with this buoyant worship, you will
gain new levels of freedom and delight. Learning to be a worshiper
will bring victory to your life.

Just think of resting in God's holiness. It will be beautiful with
no restrictions or limits. God has given you, through Jesus, holiness—you don't have to try to add anything to it. You are pure before Jesus, without any hint of sin or stain.

———◆———

I am always blown away when I think about how God has
made me—a person far, far from perfect—to be holy. Except for
Jesus, that is unimaginable. Yet it is completely true. Thank you,
Jesus. I rest in your holiness. And I worship your name and your
character.

30

Defined by Love

God will turn your weeping into joy—don't give up hope.

I've learned that his anger lasts for a moment, but his loving favor lasts a lifetime! We may weep through the night, but at daybreak it will turn into shouts of ecstatic joy (Psalm 30:5).

Your Lord is defined by love, not anger. Jesus got angry at people who used pretend faith to serve their personal interests. That is not you, and you need to understand this clearly—God is *not* angry with you. Jesus bought you and now God gladly puts aside his anger in favor of blessing you. He is delighted in you.

God's thoughts are focused on your good, on how to love on you as his new creation. He is always eager to shower his favor on you—not sometimes but always. Being in God's favor means you can be assured that you have everything you need to live a fully thankful life.

Yes, you will have times of sorrow and weeping, and sometimes those may linger for awhile. But even then, there is hope. God's promise is that you will be rescued, and you will again offer ecstatic praise to the Lord. When your time of sadness comes, remember that you are still in his favor, he is for you, and your joy will come again.

———◆———

I am hopeful because I belong to my Savior. I am learning to trust him in everything. That is the height of my life, my aim and focus. It is my rescue from sadness or despair. I know he loves me and is constantly blessing me, even in hard times.

31

Turn Distress Upside Down

God is on your side, take comfort in that as you face hard times.

In mercy you have seen my troubles and you have cared for me; even during this crisis in my soul I will be radiant with joy, filled with praise for your love and mercy (Psalm 31:7).

Coaches sometimes see small things in their players that give them hope, even though the person might be having problems competing. Coaches capitalize on these small steps to build hope and confidence in their athletes. God is far more than your coach, but you can learn from this example.

God's close attention to you is why it's possible to rejoice during hard times. God's love doesn't start and stop; it continues on when you are in pain. He knows exactly how you feel—angry, despondent, ashamed, afraid—whatever. No matter, Jesus is always with you.

Rejoicing turns your affliction upside down, just as does the belief your coach has in you. How wonderful that God knows your distress and gives you the ability to rejoice while going through it. God knows that it is best for you to get outside your issues and pain. It is good for you to praise him, even if your praise is accompanied by tears and sorrows.

The Lord knows how you feel because Jesus felt it all. He faced far greater distress than you will ever know. He knows exactly where you are, and you can trust him with your feelings.

I'm so glad to be in my Father's favor and know that he is on my side. I will hang onto him, especially in hard times. I will call on him to be my rescuer. My sorrows are real; they hurt. God's compassion is greater for he brings gladness to my life.

32

Joy of Repentance

Confession and repentance lead to your life being renewed and filled with joy.

So, my conclusion is this: Many are the sorrows and frustrations of those who don't come clean with God. But when you trust the Lord for forgiveness, his wrap-around love will surround you (Psalm 32:10).

The words confess and repent are words of rejoicing, not shame. God wants you to come to him with humility and honesty, not self-loathing. He wants the practice of confession and repentance to lead you into more freedom and happiness. Don't pretend about your sins, that is only hurting you and taking joy from your life. Not confessing and repenting leads to sorrow and sadness, not a renewed life.

God is not upset with you when you come to him in humble confession and repentance. He doesn't get tired of it—even if you are bringing him the same issue time and again. Don't hesitate and be serious about your confession and repentance.

Confession and repentance lead to real joy and a sense of renewal and new beginnings. They lead to God wrapping you up in his love. Those are great outcomes from a bad start (your sin). God makes things new, and he creates life.

———

I know it is tempting to not confess, to ignore sin, or pretend it doesn't matter. But it can throw my life off course. I will not let myself spend time in needless regret. I will be forthright, admitting my sin to God and turning away from it. I will exchange my sadness for his joy.

33

Loving the Weakest

Learn to worship God with everything you've got.

The eyes of the Lord are upon even the weakest of worshippers who love him—those who wait in hope and expectation for the strong, steady love of God (Psalm 33:18).

Isn't this a great picture—God loving the weakest of worshippers. That image produces hope and says there is room for everyone to stand in front of Jesus and praise him.

The Lord you worship is not distant or angry, but instead is very plugged into your life. He shines on you when you worship him. It's great that even those who are maybe new at worship or not yet comfortable with it, are still in the eyesight of your King. Don't worry how "good" you are at it—he is yearning to hear your worship.

Sometimes your worship is going to lift up your soul to levels you can't believe. You will be moved to tears, to laughter, to great humility, and to greater levels of trust in Jesus. And there will be times when it won't. Don't worry; Jesus loves your worship even when it feels to you like less than you want.

Just worship him. Lift up his name and his attributes. Tell him how great he is and how marvelous his creations are. Tell him how thankful you are for everything he has done for you. God loves your worship; it blesses him and lifts up your soul.

———

I used to find worship kind of boring. Wow, was I ever missing the boat! I've come now to engage in worship with all my emotions. I center my thoughts on Jesus and my Father and let the words and emotions flow out of me. Now I love worship, and it loves me back!

34

Climb on Up

The Lord is so good; climb up in his lap and enjoy him.

Drink deeply of the pleasures of this God. Experience for yourself the joyous mercies he gives to all who turn to hide themselves in him (Psalm 34:8).

Picture this—it's a hot, sweltering day, and you just finished cutting the grass. You go into your house, and there is a tall, icy lemonade waiting for you. It tastes even better than you hoped. That's what drinking deeply is like.

Drinking deeply is fully jumping in—there is no gentle sipping! And it is so rewarding. It's similar with Jesus—the deeper you dive, the more you are going to understand him, and the more the depth of his love will come clear to you. Just hanging around the edge doesn't reveal how great is his love and care for you.

The Lord is eager to give you his pleasures—peace of heart and mind, security, freedom from guilt and shame, hope in troubled times, redemption, and a life of contentment are a few of the pleasures of being his adopted child. You probably have many more in your mind.

Don't sit on the sidelines waiting for lightening to hit. Tell the Lord about your circumstances—be honest with him. Be amazed by him, adore him, and get intimately involved with Jesus.

My deep dive means I envision myself in Jesus' lap, being close and personal with him. I let the Lord be my shelter, my healing place, and my shower of relief and hope. He comforts me, destroys my past, and transforms my life.

35

Greatness of Friends

Be happy for your friends who walk with Jesus; pray for them.

But let all my true friends shout for joy, all those who know and love what I do for you. Let them all say, "The Lord is great, and he delights in the prosperity of his servant" (Psalm 35:27).

One of the Lord's greatest gifts is great friends. What a joy it is to hang around with people who will sincerely jump for joy when you get good news, and when they see you walking with Jesus. It is such a feeling of peace when you have a friend who will rejoice with you.

One of the greatest lies told today is that God is distant from or angry with you. Don't believe that for a minute. Your God, even more so than the best of your friends, takes great joy and is delighted to bring goodness into your life.

Consider a couple of your friends right now and praise Jesus for their lives. Get in touch with them; let them know that you see the Lord working in their lives. Tell them that Jesus is gleeful over their lives.

Great friends overlook your faults and encourage you. You are blessed to have such friends. If you don't, be a friend to somebody and start praying for him or her. Start slow and see what happens—chances are you will end up with a good friend.

I treasure my friends—they help make me rich. It's great to see them get good news and watch them walking with Jesus. And I know they feel the same about me, which brings me peace and makes me a fortunate man.

36

Go Ahead—Be Delighted

**Your Father knows what will delight your soul,
and he gives that to you in abundance.**

*All may drink of the anointing from the abundance of your
house. All may drink their fill from the delightful springs of
Eden* (Psalm 36:8).

When you go to certain people's houses, you know that your
welcome is going to be more than warm and the atmosphere in
that house is going to be fantastic. You can't wait to get there and
be among great friends who will bless your socks off. That's the
vibe this verse says God offers us every day. His house is full of
abundance.

Another version of this verse says that you feast from God's
abundance and are nourished by his river of delights. How great a
God that he envisions this kind of life for you! The Lord is not
skimpy with his gifts; he will never run out of good things for you.

What are some of these limitless gifts, the delights he wants to
surround you with? They are what your heart longs for—a life of
meaning and contentment. There will be peace in your life and
home. You will find acceptance, friends, forgiveness, and freedom,
and walk in hope, joy, and love. His delights are deep, fulfilling,
and authentic.

The things I want the most are the very things God wants to
pile up in my life—steadfast love, internal peace, a clear conscience,
to be loving and loved, and a lightness of being that goes beyond
description. How amazing! I am free to drink deeply of these.

37

Double Scoop, Please

You will never regret seeking more of God with all your heart

Make God the utmost delight and pleasure of your life, and he will provide for you want you desire the most (Psalm 37:4).

This great promise is kind of like going to the ice cream shop and getting to pick out whatever flavor you want or even getting two different flavors on your cone. Then when you sit back in the shade somewhere and drown in the smooth, delicious sensations of cold ice cream, you will make great memories.

As you grow to want Jesus more than anything else (making him your utmost delight), your understanding of all the Lord has for you will open up before you and astound you. That might sound a little radical, but when you make everything second compared to your desire to know the Lord more deeply, you will start to experience life in an entirely new way.

How can you grow into this? Just like when you fall in love, do everything you can to be with that person. Let the Lord light up your heart, your eyes, your mind, and your emotions. His delight is to do just that. Sit back and let yourself be amazed by who Jesus is. Your heart will be transformed to be more like his.

I want the best life I can have. I've done more than my share of messing that up, but God has turned my weeping into joy. He is turning my heart more to his, and I am loving him and my life more and more.

38

Learn to Wait

Give the Lord your broken heart, grab ahold of his hope for you.

Lord, the only thing I can do is wait and put my hope in you. I wait for your help, my God (Psalm 38:15).

Like David wrote earlier, sometimes all you have are the pieces of your life. You may wonder if they can ever be put back together again. Will you ever have reason to hope again?

Sometimes the weight of your circumstances or your sins crush you—they seem to fall on top of you and push you down. As a believer, you know in your head that all your sins have been totally forgiven, and Jesus has made it possible to experience the life he wants to give you.

But at times, your past failings can be too much, and you are overwhelmed. That's when God's hope is most there for you. You can't hope in yourself—you know yourself too well. Your only hope is in your Lord Jesus.

Thank the Lord that as you wait on him, he doesn't turn his back on you. He doesn't hold a grudge against you. Instead, his character of mercy and grace rise for you. Instead of ridicule or judgment, he gives you his compassion and peace. With those, you can face yourself and your future with hope.

Waiting can be hard, but the Lord calls on you to be patient in your hope. Pray for more "wait" in your life.

When I break my own heart, I turn to you, Jesus. I pursue you as you do me. I proclaim your victory in me and rest in the inner peace you give me.

39

Numbered Tears

**Be honest with the Lord about your feelings;
he is your great caregiver.**

*Lord, listen to all my tender cries. Read my every tear, like
liquid words that plead for your help. I feel all alone at times,
like a stranger to you, passing through this life just like all those
before me* (Psalm 39:12).

Like David, you probably face days that are filled with anguish,
worry, and tears. These problems can make you feel insignificant,
as if you aren't making any difference in the world. You need to
know that your pain is very real to God and that he does hear you
when you cry out to him.

When you feel all alone, call on your faith to tell you the
truth—that Jesus will never leave you nor forsake you. He never
even takes his eyes off you, and your tears are precious to him. He
is so close to you that he can see the meaning behind all your tears.
Jesus cherishes you, and he will bring healing to you and your
heart.

Let yourself feel your emotions; don't try to tamp them down,
hide them, or pretend they don't exist. Bring them to Jesus, who
created you to feel them. And don't isolate yourself in your pain.
Rely on trusted friends—they love you and will rally around you—
as will Jesus, your greatest Friend.

My Father is eager to take care of me. I may sometimes feel
like a stranger, like I don't matter. When I do, I will turn to Jesus
for the truth—that I matter beyond words, that I am his close
friend, and that he will heal me and replace my tears with his great,
overwhelming peace.

40

Your Song of Newness

God will always give you new hope.

A new song for a new day rises up in me every time I think about how he breaks through for me! Ecstatic praise pours out of my mouth until everyone hears how God has set me free. Many will see his miracles; they'll stand in awe of God and fall in love with him! (Psalm 40:3).

This verse is just packed full of life and hope. When do you need a new song? When somebody lets you down, or you let yourself down? When you need a breakthrough? His new song will be all about getting unstuck and creating newness in your life.

This chapter goes on to say God will lift you out of the muck and mire in which you are stuck and set you on solid ground, walking a safe path for you. It may be difficult for you to move ahead now, but Jesus will put you in a new place. And people will be astounded when they see what the Lord has done for you.

Your new song will come with newness of life, a new outlook, and new solutions. It will encourage you. It will bring gladness to your heart. People will fall in love with Jesus as they see and learn of the new victory in your life. How amazing is that!

When I am out of answers and low on hope, I go to Jesus. I grab ahold of the new song he has for me, and I will believe it, let it bless me, and use it to put a new face on my situation. It will give me courage to create a new future with Jesus.

41

Kindness Generates Life

God wants you to be an answer for those who need help.

God always blesses those who are kind to the poor and helpless. They're the first ones God helps when they find themselves in any trouble (Psalm 41:1).

God's heart is warmed by those who render aid to those who need it, especially those who are poor and can't help themselves. He will create happiness in the lives of those who help bring that aid. He wants that person to be you and desires to create joy in you as you help others.

People can be poor in different ways. Some are poor financially—they don't have money to buy food or take care of themselves and their family in times of sickness. Some are poor socially—they just can't seem to fit in; they feel separated and alone. And some are poor spiritually. They are stuck in sin or discouraged in their faith and looking for spiritual freedom.

It's clear that there is a call on your life to help the poor, especially those who can't create or find their own solutions. How to respond is going to be different for each person. But the Lord is going to call you to one or more of these groups of people. He will prepare your heart to warm to the groups he wants you to help. Your empathy for them will be real. Your response will also be real when you do something tangible to help the poor and helpless.

———

I can't do everything, but I can and will do what God calls me to do. His eyes are on the poor and helpless, and I am part of his answer.

42

Feel Your Feelings

**Put your eyes on Jesus, he will carry you
through your problems.**

*So I say to my soul, "Don't be discouraged. Don't be disturbed.
For I know my God will break through for me." Then I'll have
plenty of reasons to praise him all over again. Yes, living before
his face is my saving grace!* (Psalm 42:11)

Your emotions are wonderful—they were created by God for
your benefit. You can learn and grow from both the emotions that
are normally called good (happiness, hope, and so on) and those
that are called bad (sadness, jealousy, and so on). You will enjoy
some of them, learn from some, and get past others.

Recognize your emotions and don't try to deny them, but also
don't let your emotions run your life. For example, God knows you
will be angry at times, but he also tells you not to let the sun go
down on your anger—in other words, don't let anger linger. This
verse gives you a good checkpoint for your emotions. Remember,
you live before God's face, and he sees your life and wants you to
enjoy it.

Praising God comes from emotions such as joy, awe, and
thankfulness. Put on these emotions, focus on them to lift your life
and enable you to be a help to others.

———◆———

God will provide a way out for me—he will break down walls,
shove aside roadblocks, and leap with me in his arms over hurdles.
He will help me recover from discouragement. He will lift me out
through worship and through speaking words of truth over my life.

43

That's Not Fair

People may be unfair to you, even lie about you. Count on God to rescue you and your reputation.

God, clear my name. Plead my case against the unjust charges of these ungodly workers of wickedness. Deliver me from these lying degenerates (Psalm 43:1).

We all know that life is not fair. You've probably heard that many times. You've also probably experienced unfair treatment from people you know, people you don't know, and from the systems that you run into.

You've also seen that people who don't honor God or his people seem to get along in life better than those who walk with Jesus. That may be true, but it is temporary. Trust God to rescue you. Cling tightly to him; he will restore your reputation, your friendships, and your joy in life. And remember, you have life and live in grace and mercy. Those without God have none of these.

Your great hope in the midst of this world is in the God who walks with you. He is near when you are being treated unfairly. As David did here, call out to the Lord. Put your hope in him and don't let your emotions take over and run your life. Call on him to calm your heart and direct your decisions. Call on him to surround you with truth. This can be tough, it will exercise your faith and courage, but remember the Lord is on your side.

———

Only the Lord can give me the vindication I seek. I may have to go through some rough times before my rescue comes, but I will not give up seeking God's deliverance. I will continue to believe that he holds me in his arms.

44

Radiant Power

**God will win for you to prove that he delights in you.
He is crazy over you.**

*Our forefathers didn't win these battles by their own strength
or their own skill or strategy. But it was through the shining
forth of your radiant presence and the display of your mighty
power. You loved to give them victory, for you took great delight
in them* (Psalm 44:3).

Can you believe it—the Lord is madly in love with you. It's
not a little in love, but totally-out-of the-world in love with you.
He is filled with glee at the thought of being able to bring you joy
and peace and help you overcome your past with his grace and
mercy. He wants to give you a great life, right now.

Your battles, though probably not physical, are real. Practicing
forgiveness, choosing to live by faith, choosing to love those who
don't love you—those are all giant hills to climb. And Jesus will
truly make you victor in all of them. Rejoice that you are treasured
by a God like that.

David's armies came into battle fully prepared. You too need to
be ready. The super thing is that your preparation will be a pure joy.
Spend time in his word, pray, worship, listen for his voice, and let
his face shine on you. You will experience God's delights as you engage in these preparations.

As I learn to look more and more directly into Jesus' face, I see
that his eyes sparkle with his love and delight over me. God not
only loves me but get this—he *likes* me too. He gets a kick out of
spending time with me. Who I am brings God gladness. Imagine
that!

45

Only Pure Good

**God reigns to bring uprightness in the face
of your tears and fears.**

*Your glory-kingdom, O God, endures forever, for you are en-
throned to rule with a justice-scepter in your hand!* (Psalm
45:6)

Think of the greatest times of bliss you've ever had. It's hard to
hang onto those memories, but when you bring them up, they
create great joy in you. Life in that moment is kind of what David
is talking about here. The best you can remember or imagine is
what God's kingdom will be like for all time!

In some ways, that is beyond thought, yet that is the awesomeness of Jesus. What guides his actions? Simply put, God is good.
His character is pure. He acts by doing right. He will never bring
evil to you, never mistreat you, mislead you, manipulate you.

God wants only what is good for you. When you are walking
with God, you can lay down at night with confidence that the King
of the universe loves you always. But what about when something
bad happens—cancer, divorce, alienation from friends—what then?
God is always about bringing redemption from the bad things that
happen to us.

Sometimes that redemption is easy to see and quick to happen.
Sometimes not. Some redemptions might not happen until we see
Jesus face to face. But no matter what, keep trusting that the
Father who loves you without condition is working on your behalf.

———◆◆———

God is full of right behavior to me. When I'm facing tough
times I will, by faith, trust that he is working to bring uprightness
to my life. My best will always be found in God's character.

46

Undiminished Authority

Run into the Lord's safe place. You will find rest and strength there.

God, you're such a safe and powerful place to find refuge! You're a proven help in times of trouble—more than enough and always available whenever I need you (Psalm 46:1).

I have a great memory from a sermon once. Not because of the sermon, but because the pastor mimicked running into God's strong tower (refuge). That is a good picture of what this verse is talking about—we can run straight into his refuge.

Of course, if you are running, you are most likely in some kind of trouble. The Lord knows that these circumstances will come into your life. You don't need to live in fear about tough times (though sometimes you might want to run fast). Other believers have been in your same spot.

Jesus' power and authority are not diminished in your problems. In fact, the Bible says his strength is made perfect in your weaknesses. God is not afraid of your faults; he actually uses them to build your character and your life.

God's refuge and strong tower is a place created for you to escape to, to catch your breath, to prepare a plan, or just to find peace by being before the Father. God will be your peace when your world is crumbling and full of uncertainty.

Later, you will emerge from his refuge with confidence that your God will lead you into victory over your troubles. He will help you attack your problems from a position of renewed strength.

I don't hesitate to run into God's refuge. He welcomes me there any time. I let God's strength take away my burdens and renew me.

47

Joy Givers

**Hold your King in awe in all things
it will make your life more meaningful.**

*The Lord God Most High is astonishing, awesome beyond
words! He's the formidable and powerful King over all the
earth* (Psalm 47:2).

Two things in life are sure joy-givers: worship and thanksgiving. This makes sense, since these are like cousins to each other.
Joy pulses off the page as you read about our King, the Lord Most
High. Ask the Lord right now to fill you with his presence and
bathe you in the full knowledge of who he is. He is breathtaking in
his wonderous character.

Acknowledging God as your most high means that there is no
one or no thing that is above him. He rules over you because he is
your Creator. Without his rule and voice, everything you see
around you would fall apart.

As your King, the Lord is responsible for you. Your role is to
follow his voice, his is to find safety and peace for you, to give you
all you need to live a full and amazing life. His joy is to continually
surprise and delight you as you love him. When you put the Lord
at the forefront of your heart and mind, you will experience so
much happiness, peace, contentment ,and joy—you will find yourself full of life!

The more I hold Jesus in awe, the more loyal to him I will be
and the happier I will be. He is fully worthy of all my worship. I'm
in love with him, and with the inner life he is giving me.

48

It's Not About You

The Lord inhabits your soul, worship his mighty name.

The fame of your name echoes throughout the entire world, accompanied with praises. Your right hand is full of victory (Psalm 48:10).

Can you even imagine the depth of God's power and majesty? The name of Jesus is worshipped all across our world. People everywhere gladly follow him, lay down everything in front of him, and give him their whole hearts and lives. And the more they know him, the more they love him. Jesus never wears out or grows old to his lovers.

Worship is so cool. It's so much more than singing songs in church—you can make it into your lifestyle. Worship focuses your thoughts on the Lord—who he is and what he has done and continues to do. Worship takes your mind and focus off yourself—and isn't it great to not be so concerned about yourself all the time! And the best—worship brings you right into the presence of your King (the Bible tells you that the Lord inhabits your praises).

Focus your praise on God's character, actions, promises, and beauty. Be surrounded by the Lord and his love that resides in your life. You will walk around all day in the continual nurture of Jesus.

God's power is always at work in me and around the world. No matter what is happening to me, I know that God's name is being spoken and worshipped in every country in the world. I will walk in victory in his power and praise.

49

Power to Live Alive

**God has already given you everything you need
to live a victorious, free life.**

*But I know the loving God will redeem my soul, raising me up
from the dark power of death, taking me as his bridal partner*
(Psalm 49:15).

There is power in the name of Jesus—power to lift you out of
places where you are stuck, power to free you from addictions,
power to give you love for the difficult people in your life. His
power has guaranteed your eternal life and resurrection. The Lord
has ransomed your soul. God is now and will forever dwell with
you. You will be glad to have him in your house because you will
know him and his love completely.

This is a big deal—knowing that your sins have been wiped
away and that you now have the power to live the life you've always
wanted to. You are not powerless or trapped—Jesus has made you
free. You have the power right now to be the person you envision,
to live your dreams, and to be renewed every morning with God's
grace.

As the groom eagerly waits to see his bride, so God eagerly
waits to pour out all his best on you. His love is pure, not based on
how good you act or how you perform at certain things. So, rejoice
in the freedom that love gives you.

———

I call on God's Holy Spirit to fill me every day with wisdom
and joy, and to guide me in everything that is in front of me. I
count on him to pour out all the power I need to live fully.

50

Your Joy Engine

Practice being thankful, it will rev up your life like nothing else.

The life that pleases me is a life lived in the gratitude of grace, always choosing to walk with me in what is right. This is the sacrifice I desire from you. If you do this, more of my salvation will unfold for you (Psalm 50:23).

With God, there is always more. Experiencing more of his salvation means more freedom, more happiness, more thankfulness, and more peace of mind. Dive into the "more's" the Lord has for you by being thankful and walking with Jesus. No matter what is happening in your life, choose to be thankful.

That's easy when things are going well, but not so much when they aren't. God describes this gratitude as a sacrifice. Sometimes you need to get past how you feel to be thankful to God, not for what is happening to you, but in the midst of what is happening. It's like an engine—the more gas (thanksgiving) you give in your life, the more you will experience what God has for you, even in those times when you have plenty of reason to complain.

Thanksgiving in your life will produce joy. Your life will be better, and you will be happier and more at peace when you practice being thankful no matter what is going on. You will learn to trust God more, which will bring forth more hope and more joy. Your life will be like a joy engine!

———◆·◆———

I thank Jesus for his great gifts to me. I will practice being thankful in all situations. Lord, help me remember to thank you, especially when I don't feel like it.

51

Delighted by Restoration

**The Lord always wants to restore you to him;
he waits eagerly for you.**

*The fountain of your pleasure is found in the sacrifice of my
shattered heart before you. You will not despise my tenderness as
I humbly bow at your feet* (Psalm 51:17).

These words were written as David experienced the grief and
heartache caused by his sins. For a while he tried to hide his sin—
just as we are all tempted to do—but he was confronted by a
prophet who called out his sin. David was then face to face with
his sin and felt devastated.

Like David learned, and you too probably have found, you only
end up hurting yourself worse by being defiant or trying to ignore
or explain away your sins. You can't keep on sinning and live the
kind of life you want. Allow yourself to be broken by your sin, so
that you confess and repent from it.

David's sins were great—rape and murder! Yet when he con-
fessed, he received mercy from God. He yearned to be cleansed
and healed, and he was, even though later he did pay a big price for
his actions. God hungers for you to live in the joy of your forgiveness. Let him do that by humbly and respectfully confessing your
sins to him.

The Lord delights in my restoration. If guilt keeps me from
being humble before God and confessing, I know that is from
Satan, not Jesus. So, I will confess, I will turn away from my sin. I
know that God has already forgiven me, so I will forgive myself.
And I will do what I can to restore relationships that have been
damaged by sin.

52

Secret Sauce

You can thrive even in bad times;
soak in God's passionate love for you.

But I am like a flourishing olive tree, anointed in the house of God. I trust in the unending love of God; his passion toward me is forever and ever (Psalm 52:8).

David is under great duress, having been betrayed by an evil king who wanted to kill him. In those times, when a king wanted you dead, you were in big trouble. But look how he describes himself—as a flourishing olive tree. How is that possible?

David's secret is that he knew the real King and had his eyes and trust focused on the Lord of the universe, not the strutting king that was after him. Isn't that a great lesson in perspective. Keep your eyes on Jesus, especially when things look rough. After all, you know that he is your only hope for rescue!

David could prosper because he planted himself in the midst of God's abiding love for him, tapping into the emotional love he knew God had for him. Even though that king was still trying to kill David, he didn't let that take over his life.

Remember that God is always good and strong, look to him and wait on him. Don't wait alone—seek the presence of godly friends. Be trustful and thankful when waiting. Ask God to show you his passionate feelings for you.

———

I can succeed even in very hard times. I trust that God has a good path set out for me and cares for me more than I can imagine. I will soak my roots deeply in him and wait for him with great expectation that his mercies will carry me through anything I face.

53

God's Craving

Only God offers your life the hope you need—dig into him!

Only the withering soul would say to himself, "There is no God for me!" Anyone who thinks like that is corrupt and callous; depraved and detestable, they are devoid of what is good (Psalm 53:1).

If this is you, don't let yourself stay in this spot. God is there for you; he craves for you to call on him. He knows that once you get a glimpse of who he is, you will fall in love with him. God desires with all his heart for you to come to him.

In another translation, people who think like this are called fools. Why? Because they willingly go against truth, choosing their own path, even knowing or sensing that God's path is much better. That describes everyone at some point. But it's one thing to occasionally act foolishly and another to make it your lifestyle. Such rejection of God wreaks havoc on your mind, your will, and your emotions.

But worst of all, it cuts you off from God's goodness and from living a full, free life. You won't have an awareness of the peace and hope that God gives so generously, nor understand grace and mercy. If you know people like that, pray for them and love them; don't judge them.

———

Much of the world lives with souls that are damaged and being crushed from rejecting Jesus. They live with false hopes in false gods—things that won't last. This makes me want Jesus more. I lay aside my hope in things, for I know they are false. I grab ahold of Jesus, putting all my hope and trust in him. I've learned he doesn't disappoint.

54

Fully Given

Give freely to God, he will rescue you.
His love always covers you.

Lord, I will offer myself freely, and everything I am I give to you. I will worship and praise your name, O Lord, for it is precious to me (Psalm 54:6).

Some of David's friends were turning against him. His response was to fall more fully on the Lord and give himself over completely to God's care. He worshiped him and blessed the name of the Lord. He chose to have God remain precious to him.

David was not some kind of super-human; he sinned like you and everyone else. He made bad decisions and was afraid. But here he gives some great advice: Be thankful, worship your King in a loud voice. Take your eyes off your problems and put them on God, trusting in his character. God's name is always good; his actions always bring rightness to you; his words bring truth to your situation.

God has no desire to limit you or stomp on your joy and fun in life. Just the opposite—he knows, way more than you do, how to bring those things into our life in fullness. He wants you to experience great joy, abundant fun, and overwhelming peace. He is for you and wants to make your life better. You will be happy to give yourself fully to him.

———◆———

I will give to God freely—of my time, my finances, my worship, my skills—both when thing are going great and when things are a big mess. I know he will rescue me when I come to him. He knows where to find me because he never takes his eyes off me.

55

Take My Junk

**The Lord can't wait to take from you what you don't want,
so give him your cares.**

*So, here's what I've learned through it all: Leave all your cares
and anxieties at the feet of the Lord, and measureless grace will
strengthen you* (Psalm 55:22).

Do you ever want, just for a little while, to hang onto some of
your burdens, to be the aggrieved one, the put-upon person? You
get the choice to be that person whenever you want. But experience has taught you the rewards are bad: anger, bitterness, judging,
disappointment in yourself—a big list of junk!

Your other choice is to be honest with Jesus about your hurts
and disappointment, the times when you were betrayed or shoved
off. Give up the attempt to stew in your juices so others will feel
sorry for you. Try this instead: hold out your hands to Jesus, name
your problems to him, and ask him to take them away. Then ask
him to tell you want he wants to give you in return. You won't have
to wait long to hear or sense what he will give you—things like
peace, relief, forgiveness, a clear conscience, freedom. You can get
rid of your junk and get blessings in return.

Your burden might not disappear. You might still have trouble,
but you will now be equipped and in the right frame of mind to
handle it. You can have peace and sound judgment in the face of
betrayal.

———◆———

Another way to deal with burdens is to ask God for the opposite of what you feel. I can ask for peace when I feel anxiety and
forgiveness when I feel anger. I get release and freedom doing this.

56

Tears Redeemed

The Lord will make sorrows and tears count for good things in your life.

You've kept track of all my wandering and my weeping. You've stored my many tears in your bottle—not one will be lost. For they are recorded in your book of remembrance (Psalm 56:8).

You can be sure that your Father knows what is happening to you, even when you are filled with sorrow. The truth is that his eyes never leave you. This verse shows that he sees and keeps track of what is going on in your life. Jesus is not some far off casual observer. He is right there with you in everything you go through.

He is able. He gives you strength and truth to help you find a way through your problems. He knows you are searching for solutions, for meaning and understanding, and for restoration. He doesn't let anything happen to you without his care written all over it.

God's love is so tender, he captures and stores all your tears, and none of them will be forgotten. Imagine the comfort he will give you when you see him face to face. Even now you can take courage from knowing that he sees you and that you are not alone. Reach out to him in your pain, let him hold you in his arms, open your heart to his comfort—it is real.

I know God values me and that my problems and griefs are well known to him. My tears are not in vain—he keeps track of them for a purpose, even if I don't understand it. I believe he will redeem them for a great purpose in my life.

57

The Might of Mercy

Ask God; he will send angels to fight on your behalf.

Please, God, show me mercy! Open your grace-fountain for me, for you are my soul's true shelter. I will hide beneath the shadow of your embrace, under the wings of your cherubim, until this terrible trouble is past (Psalm 57:1).

Mercy means we don't get some punishment we deserve to get. Mercy has been revered through the ages— Shakespeare recognized the value of mercy, saying it comes gently from heaven and it blesses the one who gives it and the one who receives it. How true!

God's mercy is huge and powerful. You cannot live your life without it, and like God's grace, it is an unearned gift to us. We pray to the God of mercy for mercy—the Lord is in the business of making mercy happen for us. Mercy and grace are tied together like twins, and they both lead directly to the shelter of the Lord.

God's embrace is flowing with both mercy and grace. It is a great place to go when you need anything. You can, like this verse says, hide in his embrace. He will guard your soul from the dangers you face. In his embrace you can count on the Father sending his angels to protect you and battle on your behalf. Your soul is beyond precious to the Lord—he will go to great lengths to ensure your safety.

I count on and believe that God is constantly pouring out his mercy and grace on me. He will send angels to help me—they will go to war on my behalf. God will always be faithful to me, even when I'm not faithful to him.

58

Despise Evil

Hate evil, you can bring it to ruin.
Love the righteousness that Jesus has given to you.

The godly will celebrate in the triumph of good over evil. And the lovers of God will trample the wickedness of the wicked under their feet! (Psalm 58:10).

There are people who are evil, and this chapter is very descriptive in dealing with them. We have evil in our days too—think of terrorists or people that abuse children—God sees their acts as evil. It is right for you to want good to triumph over evil and evil to be defeated.

God calls on you (and all believers) to defeat evil acts, not evil people. God also wants you to be involved in helping everyone, including those you see as evil, to repent and accept Jesus as their Lord. Let the Lord deal with those who practice evil. For you, cherish the righteousness that God has draped over you.

None of us know how God judges on the earth, and it is not yours to know. You can know that Jesus' righteousness has become yours and will be rewarded on earth (with a life of joy, peace, hope) and in heaven (with a life forever lived in the presence of the Father, Jesus, and the Holy Spirit).

I don't have to wait for eternity to experience God's righteousness. I get that now through God's Holy Spirit and the gifts he gives to believers. I get that now in having a clear conscience and a light heart. I know all my sins and the evil stain they left are permanently wiped away.

59

Surrounded by Strength

**Jump into God's arms freely.
Your strength and safety are in him.**

*My strength is found when I wait upon you. Watch over me,
God, for you are my mountain fortress; you set me on high!*
(Psalm 59:9)

King Saul is still after David, doing all he can to have him
killed. David couldn't leave his house because of the ambush Saul
had set up. David was hiding out, watching carefully so that Saul's
people didn't sneak up on him. David knew where his strength
could be found, and it wasn't in David!

In some ways your life is like David's. Satan is said to be
prowling around seeking ways to steal from your life, to destroy
your life, or to take your life from you. So maybe David's story here
is more applicable to you than it seems.

If God is your strength, that means you don't have to rely on
your own. That's good, because many times you don't have the
strength you need. Maybe you are familiar with the verse that says
the joy of the Lord is your strength. That's good news. You have a
source outside yourself to find strength—God's joy.

From this foundation of joy you will gain strength to defeat
your enemy—to face and confess your sin, to step into a completely
new opportunity, or to face a heartbreak. Dealing with these from a
place of joy is very comforting. Joy can help you overcome whatever you face.

God's fortress is where his joy and deliverance surround me. I
will be encompassed by his peace—even to the point where I don't
understand how peace is possible. I will gain victory over my
enemy; my soul will be made safe.

60

Tender Power

God will fight for you and treat you with tenderness through your battles.

Come to your beloved ones and gently draw us out. For Lord, you save those whom you love. Come with your might and strength! (Psalm 60:5)

Are you in the middle of a battle right now, or do you see one coming your way? If so, this verse is just for you. It was written when David was right in the midst of a battle, one that was not going well for him at all.

David's army was vastly outnumbered at this point; he didn't see a way out for them, other than to call on God for rescue. David asked for two things: for protection and for the Lord to come with strength. That's a great picture. God's power and strength brought victory in a way that still protects his followers.

Sometimes you know your situation is going to require strength—maybe inner strength to resist a temptation, to find courage to conquer new ground in your career, or to find peace to deal with an on-going health issue. You need both toughness and tenderness. As David's army was rescued by Joab, so to the Lord will bring unexpected strong help for you, and it will happen with gentleness.

This story shows me that God is unlimited. His strength and might can stomp all over any foe I face. And his tenderness will shield me from harm during the fight. I will call on the Lord to defeat my enemy—to help me turn from sin, ignite a cooling heart, bring clarity to confusion and love to anger, all the while nurturing and protecting me.

61

I'm His Responsibility

**Your weaknesses, when you give them to Jesus,
become his strength in you.**

For no matter where I am, even when I'm far from home, I will cry out to you for a father's help. When I'm feeble and overwhelmed by life, guide me into your glory, where I am safe and sheltered (Psalm 61:2).

It doesn't matter where you are or what condition you are in—physically, spiritually, or whatever. If you feel far off and distant from the Father, call out to him. Don't hesitate because you feel weak, guilty, or afraid. The Lord will never, never turn his back on you. His rescue is only waiting for you to turn to him.

Crying out to God means you acknowledge you are not in control, nor are you the end-all in finding an answer. Remember, if you stay close to Jesus, you are his responsibility. That means you are willing to put your attention and hope on Jesus, not yourself or any of your circumstances or assets. You are willing to adopt a spirit of humility and thankfulness.

It means you have a goal in mind; you are in search of the next step forward. You are refusing to stay stuck where you are.

These are all wonderful traits and attitudes to have. Come to the Lord with them, and he will be faithful to you. He is unique in his love for you—no one else can do what he has in mind for you.

———❖———

Jesus is my rock; he never falters; he is always there for me. He is the source for whatever I need. I will run to him with my weaknesses; I will let him be my strength.

62

Tough Trust

**Be totally honest with God,
he is your fortress and your security.**

*Join me everyone! Trust only in God every moment! Tell him
all your troubles and pour out your heart-longings to him.
Believe me when I tell you—he will help you* (Psalm 62:8).

Trust can be hard; some people have had their trust abused or
found that some person was unable to provide the answer they had
promised. Trust is not a given; it is earned and many times has to
be re-earned. But life without trust is a tragedy. Find the right
place to put your trust.

The Lord earned your trust in so many ways; he is so worthy
of your praise and trust. The Lord is above your thinking level—he
doesn't think like you do or act like you do. God is supremely dependable and reliable. You can always count on him—he is in front
of your situation.

Trusting Jesus means that there are going to be times when
you have to choose to believe his promises and his words, even
when you can't see evidence right in front of you. Oh, believers,
those are the times that are going to bring you so much closer to
Jesus.

Trust also means you can be transparent with God. You don't
have to pretend or hide how you feel about others or yourself, or
even God himself. He won't condemn you, judge you, or turn away
from you. He will be delighted to talk with you.

I have found my God to be a refuge beyond what I could have
hoped for. He is so trustworthy; his desire for me is way above my
imagination. He is so personal and quietly loving to me, crafting a
great future that is uniquely mine.

63

In the Depths

Rekindle your passion for the Lord
by getting close to him and hearing him.

*O God of my life, I'm lovesick for you in this weary wilderness.
I thirst with the deepest longings to love you more, with cravings in my heart that can't be described. Such yearning grips my
soul for you, my God!* (Psalm 63:1)

We all face times in the wilderness when our lives are dry, our
emotions parched, and our hope feels scorched. Don't be anxious
when you are in such a time; it will not last.

Acknowledge that the Lord is the foundation for your life—
say it out loud to God—your words can help bring life to you.
Don't hesitate to expose your feelings and worries to Jesus. Crying
out to him shows the depth of your trust and the earnestness of
your plea. Be emotional—just look at the emotions David dis-
played. He talked of being lovesick, of his deepest longings, the
cravings in his heart, the yearning in his soul.

Be confident that the Lord loves to hear you talk like that. He
hasn't distanced himself from you. Sit down next to him and relax,
rest in peace, and let him minister to you. Listen to his quiet words
in your heart and soul more closely and longer than you might usu-
ally do. Jesus will bring you out of your desert place; he will refresh
you and nourish you. He will bring delight back to your life.

Waiting can be hard. But I've found that when my relationship
with Jesus isn't where I want it to be, I need to rest with him, feel
and hear his presence. I pray that God will increase my yearnings
for him, and he answers.

64

Reputation Defender

Count on Jesus to defeat all your enemies.

Then all will stand awestruck over what God has done, seeing how he vindicated the victims of those crimes (Psalm 64:9).

Maybe you think you have no enemies—and most of us don't have the type of enemies David had. But you do have a chief enemy. Your enemy is Satan. You know what his job is—to steal from your life, to destroy you, and to kill your soul.

You also may have some human enemies—or at least people who don't wish you well. Your best solution for these people is to pray for them. As you get used to doing this, ask God to bless them. As you do this, one day you are going to notice that your animosity for them is gone because Jesus will have healed you.

The Lord will also bring you victory over your spiritual enemies. He has already set you free from them through the power of his blood. You might still be stuck in cycles of bad habits or guilt and shame over past events. Confess your sins and turn away from them. Your steady obedience will keep you from being a victim to sin.

I am in awe of how Jesus has done so much for me. He has given me so much I don't deserve. The foundation of freedom from my enemies is the love the Lord has for me. God is totally on my side, and he will let nothing get in the way of that. I thank him all the time for his rescue.

65

Contented with Goodness

**Ask and God will pour his kindness all over you;
let him draw near to you.**

*And your priestly lovers, those you have chosen, will be greatly
favored to be brought close to you. What inexpressible joys are
theirs! What feats of mercy fill them in your heavenly sanctuary!* (Psalm 65:4)

This is *you!* You are the one chosen to be called blessed. Jesus
has brought you near to the Father, and your real dwelling place is
in his temple courtyard. That's not sometime in the future but
right now. You are a living advertisement for Jesus, abiding with
him.

Being chosen doesn't make all your problems go away, but it
does mean that you have constant access and even intimacy with
the King of kings. That's why you are called blessed.

You are learning how to be satisfied and content with the
goodness of the Lord, even in your bad times. You are seeing real,
honest-to-goodness victory over sin and life affirming hope over
grief. You are finding that Jesus is completely true to you and dis-
covering that he is indeed your only lifeline!

You know that real satisfaction is not found in your stuff.
Things won't give you peace in your heart or satisfaction in your
soul. You know only Jesus can make you completely comfortable.
Only he can destroy any shame and guilt you feel and elevate you
to living in outright freedom.

Being surrounded by the goodness of the Lord isn't some far-
off dream. It's my reality. Every day I put my trust in him. I will let
myself be drawn close to God; he will pour out the Holy Spirit on
me and produce joy in my life.

66

Ouch, but Thanks

God will refine you—it might be hard,
but it will set you free.

*O Lord, we have passed through your fire; like precious metal
made pure, you've proved us, perfected us, and made us holy*
(Psalm 66:10).

Life is not easy for anyone, believers included. In this verse you
see that you are going to be refined by the Lord. Does that mean
the Lord brings trouble into your life? The answer is a resounding
no! He is your loving Father and he is always good. While he
doesn't cause problems, he does help you deal with them. His fire is
rescuing you from the broken world you live in.

Refining produces purity and beauty by removing things that
actually mar your purpose. The process of being made pure can be
painful—it may not be easy on your soul. You can choose to say,
"No, God, I don't want to go through that," which will produce a
life lacking in beauty and purpose, a life that doesn't end up
counting for much.

When you say yes to God's refining, he will change you in the
manner he knows is best for you. So, don't shirk away from it.
There may be sorrow in the process, but as your refining is being
completed, newness will begin to surround you. You will experience
new breakthroughs and have more peace in your soul.

There is no shame in being refined. In fact, there is glory
through it. I am being made new and beautiful. I will let God refine
me, and he will be gentle, even if the refining is hard. He is doing it
because he wants for me the very best life I can imagine.

67

Obedience Brings Gladness

A heart that obeys the King will result in gladness and joy.

Then how glad the nations will be when you are their King. They will sing, they will shout, for you give true justice to the people. Yes! You, Lord, are the shepherd of the nations! (Psalm 67:4)

This verse is so filled with the beauty and amazing wonder of God's plan. The world shouts out at you that obedience is subservience, and it puts you in shackles. God tells you that obeying your King will create a glad heart, jubilation, and true justice. He says that your obedience will lead to a life of joy and freedom.

When you obey, you put yourself under the authority of Jesus. Maybe that thought is kind of scary—what will happen when you surrender control to him and actually make him your King? Will you be boxed in and lose control of your choices? In truth, He will use that authority to make your life better and to help you be who you really want to be.

You see, in addition to his being your King, God is also described in this verse as your Shepherd. It is a joy and comfort that Jesus is both of these. You are protected by a mighty king and a personal shepherd. Nothing is too big or too small for your Lord.

———◆———

Over time I think my life looks like my heart. My heart in rebellion will take on a demanding, negative tone. My heart that is willing to live under his standards and protection will take on a glad tone and will be a joy to me and the people around me. That's the heart I want.

68

Majestic in Everything

**Your king, who is filled with majesty,
will come to you wherever you are.**

*Let them sing their celebration songs for the coming of the cloud
rider whose name is Yah!* (Psalm 68:4)

The Psalms continually encourage believers to be very vocal in
their praises to the King. You will be blessed when you are an out-
loud worshipper. Put all your heart into your worship. Don't be
afraid to shout out joy or shed tears. Exalting people praise Jesus
with abandon, lifting your hands before him in thanksgiving. He is
worthy and amazing!

The image of the Lord riding in the clouds brings great images
to mind. Here he is riding with purpose in the sky, where everyone
can see him—what an image! In John, we see the disciples lost in a
boat, in the middle of a very large lake, in a big storm, in the
middle of the night. Yet Jesus walks directly to them! There are no
circumstances that can stand in his way of finding you.

The Lord is majestic in all of his actions—he commands your
attention. Imagine a king riding in the air with songs surrounding
him—all eyes will be fixed on him. Multiply that by a billion, and
you have a picture of King Jesus riding to us in his glory! He is
worthy of all the praise you can muster!

It's fun to imagine the Lord in situations like that. I know that,
in reality, my God is way, way bigger than I can dream or
imagine—I love that about him. Jesus is majestic, he rides with
power and authority, and yet he knows the smallest details of my
life.

69

What Defines You

**God loves it when you, in your needy state,
come to him. He will unchain you.**

*For Yahweh does listen to the poor and needy and will not
abandon his prisoners of love* (Psalm. 69:33).

In this chapter David sees himself being a prisoner in two
ways. First, he looks at his own life and admits that he is a sinner,
and he is concerned that other people may disdain God because of
his own sins. And then he sees himself surrounded by those who
have abandoned him, who despise him and offered him no help
when he needed it.

We are all needy, and like David, your life has been, and maybe
still is, full of folly and sin. If so, please be like David and turn to
the Lord, admit your sins to him, and be lifted up. Your sins don't
define you—you are an adopted child of the King, whom the Lord
has totally forgiven. He calls you blameless and righteous.

The Lord knows that you are sometimes in a kind of jail due to
your own actions. He has every right to be angry with you, but instead, he deeply desires that you gain freedom from your self-made
prison. When you call out to him (he is eagerly waiting for you), he
will break you out. He wants your repentance to fill you with hope
and peace.

—◆—

I am not ashamed to be needy. I desire to express my total
neediness to the Lord, who loves me just as I am. I have been made
free from sins that had captured me. I want God to work in other
areas, even ones I don't yet recognize. I hunger for him to act in my
life.

70

Protect the Mocked

**Don't join company with a scoffer, it will bring you down.
Come to the rescue of those who are mocked.**

*Scoff at every scoffer and cause them all to be utter failures! Let
them be ashamed and horrified over their complete defeat*
(Psalm 70:3).

You probably know some scoffers—people who are devoid of
good ideas and try to make up for that by ridiculing and casting
doubt on others and their ideas. They know in their hearts that
they are not up to being a leader and gain comfort in bringing
harm to others. People have been acting like that for over 2,000
years. And they will be around generations from now, trying to pull
others down.

David tells you to give scoffers the same medicine they are
giving you, and he calls on God to bring them to shame and total
defeat. Your challenge is to figure out how to deal with a scoffer in
a spirit of love. How would you want someone you scoffed at to interact with you? Would you want to be called on the carpet in front
of others? Or would you want to be dealt with in privacy, in a spirit
of helpfulness. It's worth a try; if it works, you've gained a friend. If
it doesn't, just try your best to stay out of that person's way.

It is so easy to scoff at ideas put forth by others. Doing so
makes me small and petty. Instead, I will try to improve an idea
and encourage the person who had the idea. I believe the Lord
would want me to come to the aid of a person who is being scoffed.
I can do some real good that way.

71

Upon Further Review

Don't sit on the sidelines.
Find your sweet spot and serve others.

God, now that I'm old and gray, don't walk away. Give me grace to demonstrate to the next generation all your mighty miracles and your excitement, to show them your magnificent power! (Psalm 71:18)

Perspective is an amazing thing. In his later years, the writer asks God to be able to show younger people God's miracles, excitement, and power. He is no longer on the battlefield, asking the Lord to bring utter defeat to his enemies. Does he still have enemies? Sure, but he looks at his situation differently now.

That is a great lesson you too can learn. You can begin to see things from a different angle—mainly how Jesus sees things. People will become more important to you. Bringing them grace instead of battle will seem smart to you. Talking with your neighbors about the Lord's love will be more rewarding than trying to keep up with them.

No matter your age or how long you have walked with Jesus, you can learn the value of repeating to others the victories God has given you. You can lift up his name and demonstrate thankfulness in all things. You can offer grace and mercy in place of competition or judgment. The Lord will give you different strengths for different times in your life. No matter what your age, get off the bench and into the game of bringing the goodness of God to others.

Ha! It's true that I'm gray, but I don't consider myself old, though my grandchildren probably do. I've gained perspective, and I've gained time to read God's Word and pray. I've never felt closer to Jesus because I see him more clearly now.

72

Uplifting Humility

Seek being modest before the Lord.
He alone is your strength.

May the poor and humble have an advocate with the king. May he consider the children of the poor and crush the cruel oppressor (Psalm 72:4).

This verse is so rich. Although written thousands of years ago, it has deep meaning and significance today. Some of you reading this might be poor financially. You may face a continued pattern of difficult choices and issues. Others—really all of us—are called to be poor in a spiritual sense.

Jesus said that the poor in spirit will be blessed. He didn't say that the poor are blessed or that the rich are blessed. He focused on the condition of a person's spirit. And even then, he didn't say that the people who are super-confident in their spiritual condition are blessed. He said those who are poor in spirit are.

To be poor in spirit is to know that you are not self-sufficient. It means there is no pride related to your salvation or growth in the Lord. Take no claim or credit in any of that. Without Jesus, you have nothing. You can't make yourself grow, nor can you free yourself from any roadblocks you face. But because of Jesus, you have a voice with the King, who is eager and ready to hear you and respond.

I humbly accept that I am completely dependent on my Lord for spiritual prosperity. He is my only hope for forgiveness and growth. And I humbly thank him for his unending gifts, for Jesus and Holy Spirit, who lives in my life and is continually renewing my mind and my heart.

73

Overcoming Failure

**The Lord will never let you down—
be hungry to be near him. Rest in him.**

*Lord, so many times I fail; I fall into disgrace. But when I trust
in you, I have a strong and glorious presence protecting and
anointing me. Forever you're all I need!* (Psalm 73:26)

A funeral was held for the mother of a good friend. This
woman had walked faithfully with Jesus for many years and was
the epitome of grace. Yet, she wrote these words to be read at her
funeral: "Lord, I have failed you so many times, but you have never
failed me." She captured beautifully what we all know about ourselves—that at times we have all not done what we wanted.

But the great news that follows is always astounding—no
matter the disgrace you face or the number of times you have
fallen, the Lord remains in you with his strong and glorious presence. He continues to watch over you and his hands-on blessings
never stop. He continues to pour his oil of gladness and forgiveness
over your life.

Believer, keep coming back to Jesus, no matter what your condition, or how you feel about yourself. In Jesus, you have assurance
of acceptance and even on-going blessings. You always have reason
for hope. Don't stay in your sin—Jesus is yearning for you to turn
back to him. He is all you need to recover.

———◆◆———

Life is not easy. So many times I have let myself, others and
the Lord down, but I declare his righteousness over me. I lay claim
to the Lord's grace and mercy, and I put my trust in him. He has
never disappointed my soul; his rescue is continuous.

74

Be Somebody's Help

**You can help set people free from sin
and the things that have trapped them.**

*Don't let these insults continue. Can't you see that we are your
downtrodden and oppressed people? Make the poor and needy
into a choir of praise to you!* (Psalm 74:21)

This verse cries out *freedom* to all who are poor, needy, and oppressed. Jesus has given you authority to have victory in your spiritual life. Recognize your weaknesses and give them to him. Learn
to use the authority of his blood to engage in spiritual battles in
your life. Learn how to gain victory over sins that trouble you. The
result will be that you will sing songs of praise to the Lord.

The Lord wants you to help financially poor people who have
few, if any, resources to help themselves. Give to the local food
bank; support charities that house and feed the homeless. Advocate
for mental health services; support missionaries that work around
the world to bring people the good news of Jesus.

Get trained in how to help those who are spiritually poor.
Become a friend to your neighbor by being friendly. When you see
them outside, walk over and talk with them. Find ways to help
them. Ask them how you can pray for them, and then do it. You
can have a strong role in their spiritual freedom.

I will become a person who helps my neighbors. I will reach
out to them, be friendly, pray for them, and do the best I can to
help them with needs they have. And I will introduce them to
Jesus, their hope for the life they want to have.

75

Careful with Your Anger

God wants to hear about your anger, but don't direct it at him.

This I know: the favor that brings promotion and power doesn't come from anywhere on earth, for no one exalts a person but God, the true judge of all (Psalm 75:6).

Experts say this verse is about God rescuing his people from an evil king, who had won many battles in cities near to Judah (Jerusalem), but then lost when fighting Judah. There was no human reason why Judah should have prevailed. The attacking king (Sennacherib) was so strong that people shook in fear of him, as if they were in an earthquake. But the true God totally defeated him.

Only Yahweh, the King of the universe can bring favor to you like that. You are being misled if you put your faith and hope in anything other than Jesus.

This chapter tells you how to get God's favor. Don't be arrogant or wicked, wait on the Lord, and don't judge. And don't raise your hand in anger at the Lord. You can be completely honest with God about how you feel. But don't go further and shake with anger at God. Bring him your anger, but don't turn on him in anger and blame the Lord for your situation.

———

God loves my emotions and wants to hear about them. But I will not direct my anger at God, as if he is to blame or at fault in some way. I will tell God I'm angry, even very, very angry. But instead of blaming him, I will give him my anger, hand it off to him, and in turn, he will give me just what I need to quiet my soul and return me to joy.

76

Unbelievable Grace

God desires your worship and thanks; those are valued gifts to him, and giving them will make your life better.

So you'd better keep every promise you've ever made to the Awesome One, Jehovah-God! Let all people bring their extravagant gifts to him alone (Psalm 76:11).

The language in this verse is very straightforward: When you make a promise to God, make sure you keep it! And while you are at it, bring God big gifts as well. Those are very high hurdles to jump over. What chance do you, or anyone, have of meeting this standard? None at all, really.

Have you kept all your promises to God? Has anyone? The unbelievable, totally grace-filled thing is that God sees you, a disciple of Jesus, to be perfect, without any sin! He has wiped away your sins and any traces or memory of them. That is how big Jesus' death and resurrection are! You may have to deal with the consequences of your sins but not with the guilt of them!

To God, you are—right now—totally dependable and completely loved. And another awesome thing is that as you grow and get closer to Jesus, you will sin less. You will learn the value of keeping your vows and promises to God. That is the greatest gift you can give him or yourself.

What extravagant gifts can I bring to the Ruler of the universe? I will bring him my praise and worship. My humility. My loving and helping the people around me. The Lord purposes to bring benefit and joy to my life. That's the greatest gift he desires for me.

77

Repel the Funk

**Don't stay stuck feeling sad.
Recall your good times with Jesus and worship him.**

*Then I remembered the worship songs I used to sing in the
night seasons, and my heart began to fill again with thoughts of
you. So my spirit went out once more in search of you* (Psalm
77:6).

Like you probably are at times, the author of this verse was de-
pressed and felt distant from the Lord. He was searching for comfort and hope, trying to regain his footing. And he knew where to
look.

It is exciting to know that the first step to getting out of a funk
is easy—remember back to when times were better for you. You
can go to your phone and look at pictures of yourself and those you
love having fun. This will help you remember all the ways these
people blessed you, and you them. It will be a first step for your renewal.

The writer also recommended worshipping the Lord and
searching for him. Sing your favorite worship songs. Or play a worship album and sing along with it. Don't be bothered if you can't
remember all the words, or if you can't sing—just jump into worship, lift your soul up, and bless your King.

Seek the Lord in his word, in your imagination, and in talks
with other trusted believers.

Sometimes I get a little stuck feeling emotionally low. That's
maybe okay for just a bit, but I will not remain stuck. I will seek
the Lord in my memories, in my worship, and in his Word. I won't
worry about how I feel; I will trust the Lord to bring my emotions
along as I think about Jesus.

78

Jesus Is Ultimate Compassion

**Remember God's mercy on you.
Be thankful and praise him.**

But amazingly, God—so full of compassion—still forgave them. He covered over their sins with his love, refusing to destroy them all. Over and over he held back his anger, restraining wrath to show them mercy (Psalm 78:38).

This was written thousands of years before Jesus was born, but it still shows God's patience with his chosen people. And it points directly at Jesus as the ultimate fulfillment of God's compassion. Once for all, Jesus atoned for all of your sins—they were all dumped on his back on the cross. What Jesus did is so remarkable, so powerful, and so unique in human history that it deserves your constant wonder and awe.

The power of Jesus' sacrifice went even further. His death and resurrection removed God's anger from you. So now when God looks on you, he sees only Jesus covering you. He sees nothing that would provoke anger or punishment—he sees only your life that is whiter than snow.

That is your status now, you who love the Lord. Rejoice in it, revel in it, shout it out loud—you are redeemed, made whole and pure. Stop right now and rejoice at God's mercy and compassion.

I love that God did the impossible for me—he rescued me when I did not deserve it at all. I love to get carried away in pondering all that means for me, and I lift up his name in praise. I love to worship the Lord and thank him for the unimaginable gifts he bestows on me.

79

Use Sheep-like Trust

Be proud to be one of God's sheep, following his voice.

Then we, your lovers, will forever thank you, praising your name from generation to generation! (Psalm 79:13)

Another version of this verse uses the word "sheep" instead of "lovers." Both are great, but the word sheep brings special pictures to mind. Jesus is called our Shepherd, and as his sheep, our job is to follow his voice. As our Shepherd, he is responsible for our safety, for finding good and pleasant pastures for us. There is no better identity than being one of Jesus' people, having been adopted into his family, to know his voice, feel his love, know his compassion and forgiveness and hope.

Sheep are not known for their great intelligence. But they do know how to recognize the shepherd's voice. You don't need an advanced degree in biblical studies—all you need is to learn to hear his voice, and run to that sound, seeking your safety and your sustenance in him.

There are different ways to hear his voice: through his written words, through worship and prayer, through quietly and intentionally listening for his voice and learning to discern his words. Do these, and you will have greater and greater assurance of hearing him and living a life beyond your hopes.

My God is so majestic and caring. He demonstrates his authority over the whole universe and also his great tenderness to me. He easily rules from the mighty to the intimate. That astounds me. I yearn to hear his voice more often, and I will lean into him with purpose.

80

Armies on Your Side

God is mighty in power and commands angels on our behalf.

O God, the mighty commander of Angel Armies, come back and rescue us! Let your beaming face shine upon us with the sunrise rays of glory. Then nothing will ever stop us again! (Psalm 80:19)

Are you blown away that God sends his angel armies to rescue you? One thing about angels, whenever a person encounters one in the Bible, the first thing that person needs to be told is "Fear not!" Why is that? Because angels, in their angelic form, are not chubby little beings floating in the sky. They are mighty warriors, created to do battle for the Lord on your behalf.

The people in this verse had not been sensing the Lord's presence. We all have felt that way at times. But God never leaves you—in fact, he never even takes his eyes off you. If you don't feel God's presence, do what this writer did—call on the Lord to shine his face and glory rays on you so that you have to see him.

Then take courage from the Lord. Have confidence that with him, you will prevail. This is where your faith comes in—ask God to give you more faith and take a step forward in your situation, believing in faith that God is in front of you. He is!

I'm assured that I can do all things through Jesus. I don't need to face tough times or make hard decisions alone. Jesus is my Advocate, and he has sent his army of angels to help me. God has all the resources I will ever need. As his child, he sends them to me whenever I need them.

81

Breaking Free

God's love, power and provision will be
your rescue and your future.

I am your only God, the living God. Wasn't I the one who broke the strongholds over you and raised you up out of bondage? Open your mouth with a mighty decree; I will fulfill it now, you'll see! The words that you speak, so shall it be! (Psalm 81:10)

This verse is a life-changer. God declares that he is your only God, and he is alive. Then he shows proof—this living God continues to set his people free. We have been captives to sins we couldn't get out of our lives until God removed them from us and purified our consciences so we could live every day in freedom.

God first tells you to open your mouth and declare your freedom. And you can encourage others with your freedom story. Then God tells you about the amazing power of your words. He says you can change your future with the words you believe and declare out loud to be true.

This shows again how close God is to you. He is paying attention to you and to the words that you believe and speak. God puts his care into action for you. God will show up in power for you as you continue to put your faith and obedience in him. Your yesterday doesn't define your tomorrow!

This verse encourages me to no end. I know that God is close to me and wants my life to be great. I know that he has given me power to deal with anything I face. I know that God can fix anything I've broken.

82

Protect the Weak

Soften your heart for justice for those without power or money.

Defend the defenseless, the fatherless and the forgotten, the disenfranchised and the destitute (Psalm 82:3).

While written for judges, this verse applies to all of us. You can have a role in helping those who cannot help themselves. Doing so will please your Father and bring good into your life as well.

This chapter begins and ends with a call for everyone to rise as God takes his place as judge of the world. Only he can bring faithful and true justice all the time. God will judge rich and poor alike under one measure—has your life been redeemed by the blood of Jesus or not? If you are not sure, ask Jesus to forgive your sins and be your Savior. If you have already done so, thank the Lord for his inexpressible gift to you.

Inequality in man's laws has always been a problem. Please pray for your heart to be softened for those without justice. Pray that God changes hearts and delivers justice in our system. Urge your friends to do the same.

And bring the gospel of Jesus to all people, rich or poor. The Lord desires for everyone to put their faith in him. Pray for your friends and invite them to Jesus.

———◆———

This is a hard verse. I know God desires equal justice for everyone. Time has proven this is very difficult—in fact it is something only the living God can deliver. I will pray for his mercy and forgiveness for our country. And I will show justice in my heart and my actions.

83

Absolutely Above All

**Bow before the Lord who is most high
and worship him. He alone rules.**

*...so they will know that you, and you alone are Yahweh, the
only Most High God exalted over all the earth!* (Psalm 83:18)

This verse follows one in which the writer asks God to destroy
the enemies of God's people. War was as awful then as it is now,
and it will likely be with us until Jesus returns and makes a new
earth. Then there will be no wars, no tears, no sickness or death—
only pure joy!

God wants you to know that only Yahweh is the true God, and
that he is elevated over everything on the earth. He calls on you to
worship your God as the only God. There is nowhere else to turn
or no others that have done what our God has done.

God is a distinct being. He was not created; he is and has ever
been just as he is now. He is not a cloud or a thought. He is spirit,
and he is alive and actively involved in your life.

He is the most high God. When you lift your hands or eyes up
to him, you are acknowledging that he is above you in every way.
This is one way of honoring him, and you will be blessed. He is the
Creator of everything; he sets all boundaries and limits, all times
and outcomes.

I rest assured that my God is above all circumstances and outcomes. He is all knowledge, all wisdom. He alone decides the
course of human behavior, and everything is leading to the out-
come that he alone desires. I worship him and him alone.

84

Integrity, Not Perfection

**The Lord covers you with his grace;
he will supply every need you have.**

*For the Lord God is brighter than the brilliance of a sunrise!
Wrapping himself around me like a shield, he is so generous
with his gifts of grace and glory. Those who walk along his
paths with integrity will never lack one thing they need, for he
provides it all!* (Psalm 84:11)

Imagine yourself in this verse. The Lord is near to you but beyond seeing because the light coming from him is too brilliant.
And he has clothed you with his grace and glory, which means that
you too have a brilliance about you. He has lavished you with the
light of grace—people will see that on you.

The Lord wants you to walk in integrity. He doesn't require
perfection—he knows that's not possible for any of us. Integrity
comes from a life walk with Jesus and from continually being made
new by him. That's what is meant by walking along God's paths for
you—only there will you find integrity.

You won't be perfect, but you can walk with Jesus and follow
the path to which he calls you. And when you do, God will see that
you have all you need to live the life he wants for you, and indeed,
the life you desire for yourself. Let Jesus always renew you on this
path.

———◆———

This verse encourages me. Though my walk has been far from
perfect, Jesus is helping me walk with integrity. I will stay on the
path he has for me—it is a pleasant one filled with riches I can't get
on my own. It is like being wrapped up in his grace and glory.

85

Chocolate Syrup

Breathe in deeply God's love, faithfulness, righteousness, and peace. He will nurture you.

Your mercy and truth have married each other. Your righteousness and peace have kissed (Psalm 85:10).

God is so great, and his gifts are so wonderful. Words fail to be superlative enough! But think of how your life has been lifted up by the four characteristics in this verse. These pure gifts will produce ongoing joy, contentment, and hope in your life.

You think that you don't deserve his mercy, but God thinks otherwise, and showers his great love on you all the time. His love covers you through every mood, every day.

In season and out, when we are faithful and when we are not, when things look up and when they don't—God's faithfulness is always in action in our lives. His faithfulness covers us like chocolate syrup covers ice cream!

Is it even possible to understand that God has made you (and all believers) righteous? How can that possibly be? Only through Jesus and the depth of his suffering coupled with the heights of his resurrection.

Peace—everybody wants it, people chase after it in so many ways. People are willing to try nearly anything to get peace. Permanent peace is God's gift to you. It is secure and on-going. You have what the world is desperately chasing after.

———◆———

All these four traits are found in Jesus. They are entwined with each other. It is indescribable that I get them all—they are a gift to me. And they grow as I walk with Jesus. I will experience them more next year than this—I am beyond blessed.

86

Total Tenderness

God's care for you is abundant, ever flowing and rich.

But Lord, your nurturing love is tender and gentle. You are slow to get angry yet so swift to show your faithful love. You are full of abounding grace and truth (Psalm 86:15).

This verse is a great celebration of God's character, and it is so peaceful and reassuring. Have you ever considered that God didn't have to be that way? Being God—with unlimited power—he could have made his nature to be anything he wanted. It brings great joy to know that the core truths about our Lord are that he is good, kind, loving, redeeming, gracious, and full of mercy. Take a minute to thank him and worship him right now.

God's character directs his actions—what he does is true to who he is. For instance, he is described as being tender and gentle. His actions with us reflect that—they show great patience and large doses of love, no matter how we act or feel. His actions prove his character—he never gives up on you or stops loving you.

Everything God has for you is a gift, not things we have somehow earned. These gifts are so big you can't even imagine their scope. Yet there is no time in your life when God's mercy, grace, love, and faithfulness don't surround you.

＞＋＜

The more I praise God, the more contentment and peace I experience. That's not some theological theory—that's real life. I am going to learn to practice praising and thanking Jesus for his character and gifts, and my life will continue to bloom.

87

Your Royal Celebration

God loves to delight your soul; thank him in song and praise.

And the princes of God's feasts will sing and dance, singing, "Every fountain of delight springs up from your life within me!" (Psalm 87:7)

You know who those princes are, right? Yes, they are you. God opens wide the door to his feasts, and with joy, invites you in to revel in great happiness. God wants you to be filled with delight. The more you learn to worship him, the greater will be your delight. You will find yourself moved and emotional before the Lord. You may cry or shout aloud your praises or raise your arms and hands to him. Go head; don't hold back.

It is a great refreshment that God can bring out sudden springs of water, springs that will refresh your soul. Those springs will lift up your emotions, focus your mind, and prepare you for whatever decisions you face. You can count on Jesus to bring those springs to you when you most need refreshment, when your life is dry and dusty.

Those springs are going to usher in fun too. Singing and dancing and soaking in God will be captivating to your life. The Lord will cause springs of living water to rise up in your heart, and you will wonderfully lose yourself in loving your family, your friends, and even people you don't know.

I will sing and dance to God and enjoy with a full heart the springs of delight he pours into me. I will put my focus on him, praising and lifting him up. He will respond by bringing me more and more delight and joy.

88

Never, Never Give Up

**Turn to the Lord in your tears and despair.
Don't give up on your faith.**

Lord, you know my prayer even before I whisper it. At each and every sunrise you will continue to hear my cry until you answer (Psalm 88:13).

The writer of this psalm had social problems—he felt all alone, and spiritual problems—he felt like God was pouring out wrath on him. Overall, this whole chapter is pretty dark. But several things stand out that you can grab ahold of, in case you face similar circumstances.

The writer turned to the Lord and kept on crying out to him. Even though he felt deserted by God, he turned to him. He didn't just sit and mutter; he turned his heart, even in great despair, to the Lord.

And he cried out to God morning after morning. This man had great faith. No matter his sorrows and pains, he went on telling the Lord exactly how he felt. He didn't hide his feelings; he was honest with God. Remember that above all else, never stop turning to God in complete openness, for he is waiting for you.

But amazingly, he didn't seem to get angry with God, and he didn't lose his faith. This is a great lesson for all of us. You may face times like this, and if you do, keep turning to God.

I need to be ready to face times like this man faced. God is not afraid of my most honest thoughts. I will keep bringing them to him—especially in times of despair. I don't know how long such a season will last, but I know it will pass. I will keep throwing myself on him.

89

Nevertheless...

**You don't know what tomorrow will bring.
Be prepared—walk every day with Jesus.**

O Lord, how blessed are the people who experience the shout of worship, for they walk in the radiance of your presence (Psalm 89:15).

This is a psalm of huge opposites. For many verses, this writer is praising God. Then suddenly doubt is thrown over everything as the writer says God is not faithful, and that his enemies are prospering to no end. This shows the fickleness of life. We all know that one phone call can send us crashing into doubt, no matter how good things were just a minute before.

But in the last verse of this chapter, the writer does something amazing. In the midst of his king being in danger, of his people being mocked and under attack, he says, "Nevertheless, blessed be our God forever and ever. Faithful is our King." You have to wonder—where did that come from?

To feel and write that statement was an act of faith—believing what can't be seen. All evidence pointed to a disaster. But this writer had walked with God long enough to know that the Lord is always faithful and to be praised. When such disasters hit you, get to that place of praising God by faith, in spite of what you see in front of you.

When I get to the point where I am walking in the light of the Lord's face, when I recognize his shout in my soul, I will be blessed. This chapter makes it clear that honoring God will sometimes be an act of faith. To prepare, I will practice praising God in small problems, no matter how I feel.

90

Your Sweet Beauty

**God pours his attributes all over you;
he is your partner in your labors.**

*O Lord our God, let your sweet beauty rest upon us and give us
favor. Come work with us, and then our works will endure,
and give us success in all we do* (Psalm 90:17).

Think about the term "your sweet beauty" and what that
means to believers. This goes way beyond God's physical attributes,
though the purity of his character and the radiant light that shines
around him will be dazzling to see. God's sweet beauty is his character and the gifts his character traits carry that bring us favor.

The attributes (sweet beauty) that rise up over and over in the
Psalms are that he is steadfast love, and he is faithfulness, mercy,
and grace. He is tenderness, forgiveness, goodness, freedom, and
joy. Take a few minutes and ask God to give you insight on each of
these marks of his beauty and how they give you favor. Listen for
his responses, and you will be inspired by what you hear.

The Lord will use his sweet beauty to give meaning and purpose to your work. The favor he gives you will be unique to you
and your challenges. You will gain the kinds of outcomes that you
have dreamed about and hoped for. He will give your endeavors
success.

I love the idea of God pouring out his beauty on me. He will
partner with me to give his favor to what I do and then make it endure and succeed. I will bathe in the traits that I love the most,
soak in them, and feel them impact my life.

Steve Akerson

91

Every Single Time

Eagerly bring your prayers to the King, he hears them and will draw near to you.

I will answer your cry for help every time you pray, and you will find and feel my presence even in your time of pressure and trouble. I will be your glorious hero and give you a feast (Psalm 91:15).

You know that God doesn't always answer yes to your every prayer. But those "no" or delayed answers actually help you. What if every prayer was answered, right away, with a "yes." You could come to see God as some kind of vending machine. That could kill your faith, which would lead to hopelessness and a dreary life.

When you get a "no" answer, bring your sorrow to Jesus, and trust by faith that God heard your prayer and that his "no" is better for you than any "yes" you could imagine. Even go so far as to thank the Lord, by faith, for that "no" answer, realizing it will lead to many better "yes" answers in the future. Then, recognize the "no" as being an act of love from the Lord to you.

A "no" answer is not the end of the story. Jesus says he will be your hero and give you a feast. A feast for a "no" answer? Yes, a feast where you are in his lap, where you know hope; a feast of faith, where you trust him even when you hurt.

Many things try to crowd out God's feast—time pressures of the day, disappointments, griefs I face—the "no's" in my life. I will not let those things keep Jesus from being my hero or keep me from my feast in his presence.

92

Your Life Made Beautiful

The Lord is doing a unique and great work in you, right now.

No wonder I'm so glad; I can't keep it in! Lord, I'm shouting with glee over all you've done, for all you've done for me! (Psalm 92:4).

God's works are endless, as is his work in your life. The works he is doing in you are for you, uniquely fitted to your situation and your needs. You can be assured of these works in you when you look at two categories of his works.

First are his works of creation and redemption that encompass all he purposed to accomplish, such as the beauty of his natural creation and the miracle of your birth and life. The wonder you see when you look around is one thing, and the beauty of your redemption goes way beyond. Multiply your awe at his creation by an infinite amount, and you won't come close to the reality of the work of his redemption. There is nothing in the history of our world that can compare to what God went through to redeem you.

Second, look at the reason for his creation and redemption—his ongoing love for you. The overwhelming nature of Jesus' love-caused sacrifice for you is a spectacular display of love. It will make you glad. It will likely bring tears to your eyes and bring you joy. It is beyond measure.

I run out of words to use when I think of how magnificent God is and how amazing and mind-boggling his works are. My praise is never as deep as I want it to be, but God is overjoyed by my worship. He is beyond my comprehension, as is his love for me. I rejoice in him.

93

Holiness Covers You

Jesus has made you holy, he makes your life to be filled with beauty.

Nothing could ever change your royal decrees; they will last forever! Holiness is the beauty that fills your house; you are the one who abides forevermore! (Psalm 93:5)

We have looked at God's faithfulness and love in earlier chapters. Now we can add another of God's attributes—that he, and all his works, are completely trustworthy. His words never change; they aren't impacted by unusual circumstances, changing trends, or anything else.

That means you can totally count on his promises—they won't change as years go by. He will never turn his back on you but will continue to lift you out of the muck of life and give you a new song to sing. Those are life-creating promises!

You are safe to put your faith and hopes in God's hands. You can be assured that God will never change his mind about bringing you only good and helping you deal with and overcome the bad things that come your way. He will not abandon you to hopelessness. As you trust him, he will cause hope to grow in your life.

His holiness will always cover you. He has made you the righteousness of God in Jesus. He won't ever back down from that, no matter how you feel about yourself. God will never do any evil. And his holiness will bring beauty to you and your family for it is a holiness that is neither drab nor colorless but one that is instead filled with attraction. It will make you more appealing.

I will jump with both feet into God's holiness and beauty. I am captivated by living in more and more beauty.

94

Escape the Frazzle

Focusing on Jesus will bring peace
and joy to your scattered worries.

Whenever my busy thoughts were out of control, the soothing comfort of your presence calmed me down and overwhelmed me with delight (Psalm 94:19).

This verse describes many of us. We go from care to care, from doubt to doubt, and everything is rushing at us all at once. It's so easy to lose focus in the trap of swirling concerns. But your loving Father has provided peace-producing remedies.

You will never have no cares or concerns. The issue is in how you handle them. You can escape the frazzle and fears and be in control. It's simple, but not easy—take your focus off your problems and put it on Jesus.

Try an experiment—take three minutes now to think only about Jesus, his promises, his character, and his actions. At the end of that time, you will discover that you are in a place of calm and delight. Your problems haven't magically disappeared, but you are no longer being dragged down by them.

You choose who and what to put in charge of your life—your problems, which lead to unrest in your soul, or Jesus, who will lead you to peace and hope by reminding you that your problems are in his hands. You will be able to face your problems with a calm spirit and from a position of strength.

When I quiet myself before Jesus and focus on him, I get the calm he promises. I relax and enjoy him. The more and longer I focus on Jesus, the more peace and joy he gives me.

95

Your Grumpiness Antidote

Practice being thankful, it will lead you into worship, which will produce joy in your life

Everyone come meet his face with a thankful heart. Don't hold back your praises; make him great by your shouts of joy! (Psalm 95:2)

Here's a great way to start every day—wake up giving thanks to your King. Before you even have a chance to start thinking about your day, take a minute to thank the Lord for his presence in your life and for all that he has done for you. This habit can change your outlook on everything and everyone in your life. Being thankful will make other people want to be around you. Your soul will bless them.

Thankfulness and praise are like two sides of a coin—you can't have one without the other. Grumpy people don't praise the Father, and people who don't practice praise are not thankful. There will be times when it is very hard to be thankful. When that is your situation, start with some small bits of thanks to God and let it roll out from there. That will be a praise-generator and a joy-creator for you.

Your thankfulness and praise will bless others, and your joy will be multiplied. Practice—find any little thing and thank Jesus for that. As you grow, your worship will get more fun, and your heart will be changed.

The more thankful I am, the more I want to worship. The more worship and thanks in my life, the greater joy I experience. The more joy I have, the more people will be drawn to me.

96

Forever Breathless

You will forever be breathless at the beauty and majesty of God.

Breathtaking brilliance and awe-inspiring majesty radiate from his shining presence. His stunning beauty overwhelms all who come before him (Psalm 96:6).

Do you wonder what you will experience when you are before God's face, in his sanctuary? That's a great question to ponder—the answers God gives you will be a great cheer to you.

The Bible says that Jesus is sitting at the right hand of the Father in his sanctuary. Among other things, that means that Jesus holds equal authority with his Father. And it means that sanctuary is real, it is a tangible place where you will dwell, along with the Holy Spirit.

This sanctuary will have all the characteristics of God—it will be holy, pure, full of brilliance and praise and peace. It will display all the attributes of God, it will be a place of light, magnificence, grace, and kindness. There will be total acceptance, no judgment, no blame. Unlike earthly splendors, you will never get used to the splendor of God's sanctuary. It will take your breath away every time you look around.

God will put his majesty and strength on full display. We will see that he has no limits—he will show all his authority and sovereignty, and we will love it forever. It will reflect God's beauty, and nothing you have ever seen in your life will compare.

———•◆•———

My senses will be amazed in God's sanctuary. I won't be able to hold my praises inside; they will constantly pour out of me as I search for ways to describe how astonishing he is.

97

Don't Play with Fire

All sin is evil; turn away from it right away.
Confess and repent quickly with your heart.

Listen, you lovers of God! Hate evil, for God can keep you from wrong and protect you from the power of wickedness (Psalm 97:10).

This is very straightforward. As followers of Jesus, you are called not only to avoid evil but to hate it. There is no room for evil in a person who loves God. Hate means to have a strong, negative gut reaction to anything evil. Don't even get close to it; don't edge up to it so you can see what is going on but run from it as quickly as you can. Evil will hurt you and others around you.

Sometimes you might try to downplay sin by saying sure, it is sin, but it is not evil. All temptation to sin comes from Satan and his followers. There are no sins that are "only a little wrong" or only "a little evil." All of them put you into partnership with your enemy and put distance between you and Jesus.

Wickedness has power but nothing compared to the power you have in Jesus. Your peace of mind, safety, joy, hope, and peace are all found only in Jesus, and he will destroy any wickedness you face.

I'm playing with fire when I don't see the depth of evil in my sins. I will not settle for having any evil in me; I will hate evil and stay away from it. A great weapon will be my physically and emotionally turning my eyes to Jesus, and thinking about him, not the temptation.

98

Constantly More Freedom

**Jesus will work powerfully in you.
Love him with joy and sing songs to him.**

*Go ahead—sing your brand-new song to the Lord! He is fa-
mous for his miracles and marvels, for he is victorious through
his mighty power and holy strength* (Psalm 98:1).

Remember in Psalm 40 we are told the Lord will give you a
new song that celebrates new freedom. This verse reminds us that
Jesus is constantly setting you free. The great news is that the Lord
is famous for his miracles, and he is creating them in you every day.

Want proof? Look no further than his continual washing away
of your sins. And, also remember that it is Jesus who has released
you from shame and guilt. Jesus gives this priceless gift freely to
you. You can live in joy and peace every day and enjoy great pleasures in your earthly life.

God wants you to revel in the goodness of life he gives you.
Praise will make joy and peace well up in your soul. You will feel
him lifting up your emotions and giving you strength in your faith.
God has given you a new song—one that angels marvel at. He is
stronger than anything you face—strong enough to release you to
live in full liberty.

———

My new song is one of rescue and ongoing freedom to be who
I really want to be. The Lord paid an unimaginable price to give
that to me. I will party with him in the joy he has given me. I will
live greatly for him, continually singing new songs that thank him
for my elation in life.

99

Awe Draws You In

Acknowledge the Lord's greatness and authority.
He reigns over all.

Yahweh is King over all! Everyone trembles in awe before him.
He rules enthroned between the wings of the cherubim. So let
the earth shake and quake in wonder before him! (Psalm 99:1)

The idea of being in great awe of the Lord, so much so that his followers tremble, is slowly disappearing. What does it mean today to be in awe before God?

As a believer in Jesus, it is good for you to know that he is great above you. He is immeasurably great in every way, including his Lordship over you. It is good to bow before him, to kneel in recognition of his being your King. It is good to have a very strong level of respect and reverence for him.

It doesn't mean that he wants you to be afraid of him—remember he has adopted you and made you his child. And it doesn't mean that you should be worried that the Lord is waiting for an opportunity to slap you down—please don't ever believe that. The Lord's patience with you is infinite—having been purchased by the blood of Jesus. He yearns to give you comfort and draw you into his arms.

The Lord wants my awe of him to draw me closer to him. I want that too. I want my awe of him to help me stay clear of sin. I want my awe of him to give direction to my life and to give me courage to obey his words. I know that this kind of awe will take my life to new levels. I will be able to rest in his arms in total peace.

100

All of You

**Learn to rest in the Lord, to hear his voice.
He will nourish your soul with kindness.**

For the Lord is always good and ready to receive you. He's so loving that it will amaze you—so kind that it will astound you! And he is famous for his faithfulness toward all. Everyone knows our God can be trusted, for he keeps his promises to every generation (Psalm 100:5).

Jesus always has his arms open to you. You don't have to improve yourself; you don't have to change. You are his beloved child; all he wants is you. An earlier verse in this chapter says that God made you, and that now he is responsible for you, one of his sheep.

The promise of his kindness is breathtaking. You probably know an astoundingly kind person. Jesus is that and so much more. Nothing ever can decrease his kindness toward you—you cannot diminish it, nor can you make it any bigger than it is. It's nearly impossible to conceive of the love he has for you and how that shines out in his kindness and goodness to you.

Being one of his sheep means you are best off when you go where he directs. That is not restrictive, it is liberating and a gift to know that you are being led to places where your soul will flourish.

———————

I will stay close to Jesus, where he is able to make happen all that he wants for me. I want to live under his care in his pastures. I will move from place to place as he leads me. I will live all the days I have being renewed and refreshed.

Steve Akerson

101

Friends—Your Great Gift

**Build trustworthy friends into your life.
You need them; they need you.**

*My innermost circle will only be those whom I know are pure
and godly. They will be the only ones I allow to minister to me*
(Psalm 101:6).

Without a doubt, one of God's bests gifts to you are your good
friends. Like most of us, you probably can't imagine living without
them. They are the people who accept you, encourage you, and like
being with you. You know they are not perfect, and they know the
same about you. You trust them to live faithful (not sinless) lives
and be seeking the Lord with humility. You trust them to stand by
you when others might not.

You have a great opportunity to minister to your inner circle of
friends by being faithful to them, actively engaged in lifting them
up, praying for them, and encouraging them. Doing so will help
them live closer to Jesus. And it's heartwarming to know they are
doing the same for you.

You know from experience that you cannot stand on your own,
and you know your friends can't either. It's important to know that
they need you every bit as much as you need them. Let them know
you appreciate them and treasure them.

I will look with favor on my friends, believing and seeing the
best in them. I will seek for ways of building them up, praying for
them, being ready with a glad word for them, and letting them
know that they are loved. I will accept them and support them in
life's ups and downs.

102

Freedom Coming

Jesus will set you free, you will be released to experience life with lots of joy.

He listened to all the groaning of his people longing to be free, and he set loose the sons of death to experience life (Psalm 102:20).

Does God favor one type of person over another? Do the rich and powerful go to the front of the line to have their prayers heard? No, absolutely no! God does not respect one person over another. His regard for the outcast is the same as for a company's CEO. This writer comes to realize that his King, the Lord of the universe, does hear the prayers of the poor and needy like himself.

While many in our society look down on the outcast, the Lord isn't like us. His love for each person is overwhelming, and he is fully attentive to the prayers of all, which is good news for all of us. You too have been poor in finances, in spirit, in relationships, in health, and in hope at some time in your life. No matter your condition, Jesus is watching over you. He will release his power into your life.

Rely on Jesus' authority to help you get rid of the bad habits or sins that have you in their hold. Call them out and command them to leave in the name and power of Jesus. Keep that up, and freedom is coming your way.

⋙•✦•⋘

Jesus is always ready to pour out his power in my life. His authority and the power of his blood have released me from jails of my own making. He always hears my prayers and is acting on my behalf.

103

Overflowing Love

**God's love is very real; it will sustain you.
Learn to quietly rest in it and soak it up.**

Lord, you're so kind and tenderhearted to those who don't deserve it and so patient with people who fail you! Your love is like a flooding river overflowing its banks with kindness (Psalm 103:8).

You are God's beloved worshipper. Yet like all believers, you have been undeserving of his kindness and patience. Don't let that get you down; instead, rejoice in it! Jesus has paid in full your ticket to the Father's over-the-top kindness, tenderness, and patience. Take a few seconds now to lift up Jesus' name and thank him for his undeserved gifts.

God's grace and mercy cover you entirely. You get what you don't deserve and don't get what you do deserve. He has redeemed you, forgiven you, and now extravagantly removes your shame and your guilt, replacing them with goodness and thanksgiving.

His overflowing river is a great reminder of how patient the Lord is. We have each given the Lord reasons to be angry, but he sticks by you. Like a river his love keeps on coming in abundance. The cup of his kindness is never empty; it's unmeasurable like the stars in the sky.

The Lord is more than worthy of your worship. His character is deserving of all the praise you have to give him. You can multiply the joy you experience by worshiping Jesus.

There is no King like my Savior, Jesus. He is beyond what I can imagine or dream. Jesus, I praise you for always pouring out your unimaginable love and kindness on me. I will rest in it and trumpet it with joy.

104

Can You Imagine It?

**Bow down before your great Creator.
He is amazing, as are his works.**

*O Lord, what an amazing variety of all you have created!
Wild and wonderful is this world you have made, while
wisdom was there at your side. This world is full of so many
creatures, yet each belongs to you!* (Psalm 104:24)

God's imagination in his creation is a wonderful thing to behold. Could any of us have thought up the variety and the plan required to make it all happen? Some people believe it is all by chance, but to believe that diminishes the wonder and awe of the Lord.

Like the writer, sit back and look around in astonishment. Give God praise that he has fit the world together in such an amazing way. Praise him for his great wisdom, imagination, forethought, and power. His creation is not at all haphazard or the result of mindless, thoughtless mutations. It is the result of your Father's love.

All God's plans are purposeful, including what he has planned for you. Those plans unfold over time as you participate in life and growth. He gives you freedom to jump into what you care for the most. You won't ever know what your future holds on earth. That's okay, because you know who holds your future. And the very best things that happen here on earth will be overwhelmed by the first minute of eternity you spend with Jesus.

I proclaim that I am God's creation and a portrait of his redemption. As I walk on Jesus's path for me, I will be on a path filled with wisdom and goodness. Thank you, Jesus, for your imagination and plan that created all I see. Your goodness is beyond telling.

105

Rush of Goodness

**Do everything that causes you to fall
more and more in love with Jesus.**

*Seek more of his strength! Seek more of him! Let's always be
seeing the light of his face* (Psalm 105:4).

It is good to seek the Lord all the time for the same reasons pilots keep flying a plane—if they stop, it will eventually crash. If you stop, you will open yourself to all sorts of hurts—fear, anger, unkindness, anxiety, and sadness. You will find yourself saying things you wish you hadn't, and living in ways you wish you weren't. And you will cut yourself off from the purpose and joy God wants to give you.

Why would you stop seeking the Lord when doing so brings so much pleasure? Hearing his voice is such a rush of goodness. Feeling him soften your heart is so encouraging. Seeing his face more clearly brings so much strength and confidence. Living like you always wanted to is pure joy!

Find things that delight you in the Lord and do them. You are unique, so the things that bring you closest to Jesus will be all yours. Seek the joy of the Lord and jump into the things that bring you there. Jesus wants you to live a life of wonder in him.

———◆———

What brings me joy are worship and praying for people, so I find ways to do these things. I believe they are important in encouraging me and bringing me closer to Jesus. I also get great delight in learning to hear his voice through his written words to me and the thoughts he gives to my mind and heart.

106

Importance of Perspective

Don't be captured by your problems.
Focus on God's provisions for you.

Yet they still didn't believe your words and they despised the land of delight you gave to them (Psalm 106:24).

It was difficult to pick this verse out of Psalm 106. Verse 3 says the happiest person is the one who obeys God and lives righteously. It would be easier to talk about that verse, but because it is so real to your life, verse 24 stood out as important to dive into.

In this verse the people, despite a miraculous rescue and being fed every day, focused on their problems and completely turned their back on the Lord. We look at these people and wonder what was the matter with them? How could they be so short-sighted?

But then you think, have there been times when you have despised the land of delight he has given you? If so, how can you be different than they were; what better choices can you make?

Be aware of God's gifts to you and be thankful. Remember the times and ways he has rescued you and be thankful. Choose carefully who you listen to—don't listen to the grumblers, or the cheap substitute ideas of those who say they have a better idea than the Lord. Reject the lies that say something is better than what God tells you. Listen to the Holy Spirit in your life, his quiet voice guiding you.

———◆———

I choose to live in obedience and thankfulness. I will declare that the Lord wants the best for me, and that obedience is delight and brings gratitude, lightness, joy, and contentment to my soul.

107

Be a Repenter

Do the right thing, but when you don't, call out to the Lord in repentance.

Then we cried out, "Lord, help us! Rescue us!" And he did! (Psalm 107:6)

This short verse is repeated four times in this chapter—so it must be significant. Each time it is used, it covers a different type of problem the people were facing. Whether your problems come from finding yourself in a desert, from a time of rebellion and disobedience, from running away from the Lord, or from your life being in danger, know this: the Lord your God is always, always waiting for you to cry out to him.

It's clear that our King knows we are going to find ourselves in bad spots from which we can't see a way out. Jesus will not ignore you, even if these tough spots have been caused by your choices and behavior. God wants you to live in obedience (because he knows it is the best life for you), and he will help you do so, especially when you cry out to him in repentance.

This verse calls for you not to be stubborn, so stop digging the hole you are in any deeper. Put your eyes back on Jesus—he promises to lift you out of your stuck spot, put you on a solid path, and walk with you. Don't despair—his rescue is personal and very close.

I will turn to God in repentance. I will be humble before him. I will choose to lift up my hands and thank God for his marvelous kindness, for his miracles of mercy, and for his rescue of me.

108

What a Beautiful Morning!

God will give you victory in your life—call out to him!

With God's help we will prevail with might and power. And with God's help we'll trample down our every foe! (Psalm 108:13)

This chapter starts with David beginning his mornings with singing, playing instruments, and praising God. He did this whether things were going well or not. This practice set the tone for everything else he faced each day. His praise and focus on God gave David confidence and courage to proclaim that God was with him and his armies.

This is a great model for you. Begin each day with praise and worship of Jesus. Make requests of the Lord—ask for his help. Acknowledge that God's help will make a difference—that he is powerful enough to give you victory. Then take a stand of faith to believe that you will prevail with the Lord's help.

All this is possible because of your faith and Jesus' love for you. So, worship in faith that you are heard. Ask in faith that God will honor your request and actually change realities here on earth. Trust and proclaim in faith that God will give you victory over foes that seek to steal your joy and destroy your peace.

I have seen God do mighty things in my life and the lives of my family members. I've seen him shrink a cancerous tumor before any treatment was done. I've seen him turn a heart that had been dead to him for over 70 years to a heart that is filled with gratitude and love for Jesus and others. I've seen him set me free to live the life I always wanted.

109

Love Makes You Free

Turn your face to Jesus for solutions;
don't focus on your enemies.

But now, O Yahweh-God, make yourself real to me like you promised me you would. Because of your constant love and your heart-melting kindness, come be my hero and deliver me! (Psalm 109:21).

Again, this is written when David was in deep trouble. People were after him, hating him, and disparaging his name. It's interesting to see that David doesn't turn the other cheek here; he asks God to punish those who are hurting him.

A couple times in this chapter, David breaks free from his thirst for revenge. This is one of them, and it shows that David acknowledges his need for rescue, not revenge. And he knows that only the Lord can give him that rescue. He wants to see more of the Lord, and he relies on the proven kindness of the Lord. This is important—when you ask God for help, do so acknowledging that you are asking under his authority.

God always acts with steadfast love toward you. His love is not limiting; it is good for you, and you can trust it. It is safer and more satisfying for you to line up under God's authority than it is to try to get revenge on an enemy. Jesus would rather have you give your problems to him—he knows that is better for you.

———◆———

I will experience times that will discourage me. That doesn't mean God has taken his eye off me; it means I've temporarily taken my eye off him. I will turn back to God and focus on him. I will thank him and trust in his rescue.

110

With Jesus, You Win

The Lord is your strong friend.
He wins your battles and protects you.

Yahweh said to my Lord, the Messiah: "Sit with me as enthroned ruler while I subdue your every enemy. They will bow low before you as I make them a footstool for your feet" (Psalm 110:1).

There is a lot going on that we cannot see. In this verse, Yahweh (the triune God) is telling Jesus that he will go out and defeat all of Jesus' enemies and that those enemies will bow down before him. This same thing is said in Philippians 2:10—"Every knee shall bow...and every tongue confess that Jesus Christ is Lord." You know the final score—Jesus wins!

God knows that you will face confrontations with your spiritual enemies. Be strong and know that those enemies will be utterly defeated. Even now they are powerless against you if you face them in the name of Jesus. Know for a certainty that you can be a victor in every circumstance by relying on the authority of Jesus to conquer your spiritual enemies.

Not only are Jesus' enemies fully defeated, but they are going to be used as a kind of footstool for Jesus. Isn't that great! Maybe this language is figurative or maybe it's literal. In any case, it shows that when you put yourself under the authority of Jesus, you will experience freedom to live with a restful soul.

Jesus rules today. He is destroying my enemies. I will align myself under his rule. My safety is found in him, so I will actively put my life in his hands. I will praise him with joy, knowing that his authority makes me completely safe.

111

A Flawless Creation

**The Lord is trustworthy, and he has made
you pristine before him. He is truth!**

*All God accomplishes is flawless, faithful, and fair, and his
every word proves trustworthy and true* (Psalm 111:7).

This is a verse to fall in love with. You've seen previously that
God doesn't intend that his words should limit you. He means for
them to help you live a delightful life with ongoing joy and contentment. That shows loud and clear in this verse.

At the foundation is the truth that God is flawless. How else
could he create flawless things? His behavior to you is flawless. His
plans for you are flawless. His faithfulness to you is flawless. His
words are always true and will always guide you with accuracy and
authority. At times you may doubt that; if so, activate your faith to
believe in his perfection. It will give you courage to move ahead.

God also always acts with fairness. His behavior is impartial.
He loves us all equally, all the time. And that never changes. What
God calls right will always be right. His words over and about you
are all trustworthy. You will be continually blessed when you keep
your promises to him. You will be renewed with brand new blessings each and every morning.

———

I can hardly believe that a flawless God adopted me into his
family. And that he sees me (thanks to my redemption by Jesus) as
righteous. Those two facts are life-altering. As I remember that
and trust in them, I will never be the same person I was.

112

Fearless Living

Make the Lord your strength as you boldly face the problems in your life.

They will not live in fear or dread of what may come, for their hearts are firm, ever secure in their faith (Psalm 112:7).

Who are the "they" in this verse? The people, like you who delight in the Lord, who live with integrity, are gracious and tender. And very importantly, they are people who are generous and charitable—never stingy—and they live with honesty and truth.

That's quite a list of honorable attributes. Notice the "they" are not the rich, not the powerful, not the connected, and not the people who live with fear and try to shirk or ignore problems in their lives. They don't shrink back, don't blame others, they calmly face every foe in their lives.

That almost sounds unreachable, but it can be and maybe already is you. You can stand strong, facing the spiritual enemies that want to destroy you—you can defeat them. With the Lord, there is no reason to panic. Turn to Jesus, who is your power, and ask him to fight for you. He wants to make you a victor, and he will.

The concept of generosity shouldn't be overlooked here for it seems foundational to becoming this kind of person. Giving to others can be hard, but it is creating you to be a person of trust and compassion, traits that will help you live life fearlessly.

I can and will live victoriously through good news and bad. Jesus will never disappoint me; he will give me victory over bad habits. He will get me over roadblocks I face and make me into a generous person.

113

Like Each Snowflake

**Your Father is unique, he rules
over everything he sees, and he loves you.**

No one can be compared to God, enthroned on high! (Psalm
113:5)

What makes your God different? Why do you give him your
praise and worship? Why do you get joy from your obedience to
him? You probably have reasons that come to your mind. Here's a
starter list. As you read it, bless yourself and the Lord by praising
him and thanking him for each of these.

- He is alone in the universe—there is nothing and nobody like
  Him. He sits on high, at the top of everything.
- He is your Creator, and the Creator of everything you see—all
  the earth, the skies above and the oceans below were all fashioned by him out of nothing. The direct hand of Jesus, your
  creative and loving God, did it all. He created beauty and magnificence because he is beauty and magnificence.
- He is your Father; his heart of love and tender compassion
  fuels his desire to be close to you and have an intimate relationship with you.
- He is your Redeemer; he paid a price you can only wonder at
  to restore your relationship with him.
- He is your friend and advocate. He stands up for you and prays
  for you.

————◆————

I love to worship my Lord. An old song says, "Does he care
when I've tried, and I've failed? The wonder of wonders, that thrills
my soul, is that God loves me." No matter what is happening with
me, no matter if I've been faithful or not, God's love for me is
steadfast and unbreakable. There never has been, never is now, and
will never be anyone like my Lord, God, and King.

114

The Imagination of Jesus

The earth belongs to the Lord—
look closely and watch all he does.

Tremble, O earth, for you are in the presence of the Lord, the God of Jacob (Psalm 114:7).

An amazing thought is that the physical earth itself falls under the authority of its Creator, your King Jesus. Three quick examples: (1) The Bible says that if the people didn't praise Jesus, the rocks along the side of the road would do so. (2) The sky darkened at the appointed time during Jesus' crucifixion. (3) And Jesus only had to say the word "peace" and a storm was calmed.

It is natural and right to stand in awe of Jesus and to be overwhelmed by his creation. Think of the power and imagination of Jesus. When you are spellbound by what you see on earth, turn that awe into a blessing by lifting up your wonderous God in worship and thank him for his work. Shout out his greatness, his character, and his beauty.

God is big, full of majesty and grandeur. And yet he is very intimate and personal in his knowledge of you. He knows your joys, your fears, and your hopes. God is able to put order into the universe and do the same with your life. He causes all things to work together for your good when you walk with him.

———✦———

I thank you, my Savior, for your sure and deep love for me and for the close attention you pay to me. I thank you that you created peace, and you drape it over me. I thank you for all the works of Jesus. I will stop and be captivated by my thoughts of you, as you are by me.

115

No Other Hope

Don't let anything become more important to you than Jesus.

Dead men can only create dead idols. And everyone who trusts in these powerless, dead things will be just like what they worship—powerless and dead (Psalm 115:8).

Most of us don't have melted golden idols in our houses, nor do we bow down to any images or likenesses of a false idol. To us, it sounds ludicrous to believe such things could create life, offer forgiveness, or give hope. We might then be tempted to quickly dismiss a verse like this.

But stop a second and consider why these idols were created—was it so people could put their trust in something visible, something they could touch and see? What's the difference between those idols and things that might capture your soul, like your bank account, your job, or your house. There is nothing wrong with any of them, but if you fall into the trap of looking to them for hope, they could wreak havoc on your faith.

Things like that become idols when you place your hopes in them and count on them to provide for your future—thus they become more of a focus in your life than Jesus. You are called to be a good manager of the things God has given you, but make sure Jesus is the only place for your hope and your worship.

Something becomes an idol over time; it gradually gains prominence in my life as I count on it, instead of Jesus, to deliver for me. I will continually offer to Jesus the things that could potentially become idols in my life. I will let him own them. I will place my allegiance and faith in Jesus alone.

116

Life Worth Having

**God loves your honesty; tell him how you feel
and give thanks to him in everything.**

*Now I can say to myself and to all, "Relax and rest, be confi-
dent and serene, for the Lord rewards fully those who simply
trust in him"* (Psalm 116:7). ·

This is a life worth having—one that includes being able to be
content, happy, and calm. Those words convey a very strong im-
pression of a life of both internal and external peace, and it happens as you learn to more and more "simply trust in him." Of
course, many times we don't find that to be very simple at all, but
there is a way.

Another translation talks about offering the Lord a sacrifice of
thanksgiving. At first that sounds a little odd—how can thanksgiving be a sacrifice? But you know it can be hard (a sacrifice) to be
thankful at some points in your life. As you make being thankful a
lifestyle, it will change your mindset and your life. Start by
thanking God for one or two things every day.

Thanksgiving will also usher more humility into your life.
Giving thanks means that you are giving up the opportunity to
grumble or complain. You will gain peace when you replace a crit-
ical spirit with a thankful one, and you will be creating hope for
you and everyone around you.

———

This verse is down-to-earth real. When I face a disappointment, like a negative health diagnosis, I will take a step back and
tell God I'm thankful to him, even in (but not for) this hard news.
When I do this (I'm very much still learning), God does bring me
peace and help me rest and not worry or have anxiety.

117

Overcome by Kindness

Surrender to God's faithful love; let it fill you up.

For he has conquered us with his great love and his kindness has melted our hearts. His faithfulness lasts forever, and he will never fail you. So, go ahead, let it all out! Praise Yah! O Yah! (Psalm 117:2)

Yah is the name of God as he displays his power. It's fantastic that God chooses to display his power (and ability to conquer us) by pouring out his love, kindness, and faithfulness on us. That is so like our Father, who created us with freedom and fashioned the world so that we would be happiest when we choose to be obedient.

Think of your heart being melted by kindness—what a wondrous image! New babies and grandchildren do that. For some, pets do that. All these are precious gifts to us, we love to hold them in our hands. Try doing the same with Jesus. Lift up open hands to him and ask him to fill your hands with what he has for you. Rest and listen for what he gives you and how you feel.

You will experience his tender kindness and his comfort when you hurt, his smile when you look at him, his confidence when you face new challenges. You will hear words that encourage you; you will feel total acceptance by him. You will know that he is your personal Lord. Praise him!

God's love and tenderness for me will never falter; they will keep coming like waves on the sea. My forever started when I was made his child. Because of that, I live in his forever now. This gives me great peace and a hopeful outlook.

118

You Have Authority

You can be free from anything that has captured you, learn to use God's authority.

Out of my deep anguish and pain I prayed, and God, you helped me as a father. You came to my rescue and broke open the way into a beautiful and broad place (Psalm 118:5).

What a wonderful promise from a magnificent God! He is powerful enough to rescue you from any hole you have dug for yourself or any captivity in which you have been put. No chain can keep you bound; no jail can hold you.

A favorite verse says, "For freedom Christ has set us free." Freedom is so important to Jesus that he gives it to you for its own sake. He knows you can't have a great life without freedom, so he moves anything and everything to set you free.

Have you ever been, or are you now, not free? Are you trapped in a habit, a mindset, or an addiction to sin? If so, you know how hard it is to escape on your own. Don't worry, you are not your own rescuer—Jesus is the one who can set you free. With authority, humility, and trust in Jesus, you can be rid of that sin or addiction, no matter what it is or how trapped you feel.

—◦—

My Father has a beautiful and safe place in mind for me—one that will overcome any pains I have faced or even caused. I know he will knock down anything that gets between me and his vision for my life. My best is to place all my hope in him and walk in his footsteps.

119

Listen—God Is Talking

God's words will bring you joy
and fill your heart with pleasure.

Everything you speak to me is like joyous treasure, filling my life with gladness (Psalm 119:111).

God speaks to you in different ways—through his written Word, through quietly speaking into your heart, through worship, through dreams, and through the advice of others.

One very strong pastor friend has said that God has a lot more "talk" than you have "listen." That is so true. Your joy is to learn to listen. When you do, your life will be filled up with wonder and delight over and over again. You will experience new kinds of treasures you didn't even know were possible.

Listening is sometimes done quietly and alone via his words in the Bible. Ask God what they mean for you and wait gently to hear him. He will, without a doubt, talk to you. Listening is sometimes done loudly—God will talk to you when you worship and praise him. Listening is sometimes done with others—ask a trusted believer what words the Lord has for you and ask God to verify them to you.

Learn to listen to God; practice doing it. His words will bring richness to your soul. You will be taken by delight and a lightness of your soul. Hearing God is the greatest thing. He is talking to you right now.

God's words bring me joy. I'm excited by his words in the Bible. I'm grateful for trustworthy friends from whom I learn and who encourage me. And I'm learning more and more to listen quietly for God's words to me. They are gentle and clear. They put more life into my life.

120

Don't Believe Lies

**Reject the accusations that Satan says about you;
they are devious and full of deceit.**

So come and deliver me now from this treachery and false accusation (Psalm 120:2).

Have you had people spreading false accusations against you? Think of your family or friends being fed false and damaging information about you. The world can be very cruel, and this type of verbal abuse can be devastating. If this is happening to you, go to your family and friends with the truth and spread it wherever you can.

Whether this has happened to you or not, you have an enemy that loves to tell you lies about yourself. Satan and his demons love to try to tear you down, to pile guilt and shame on you, and to destroy your life in any way they can. They are going to try to get you to believe lies.

Don't do it! A good practice is to say out loud "I reject (whatever lie is being thrown at you)" and ask God to take them away from your memory. Renounce Satan's lies and order him to be gone, and he will run away when he faces the power of Jesus. Whenever you hear lies telling you God doesn't love you or that there is something wrong with you, don't buy into them, reject them, and send those words away.

I am the righteousness of God in Christ Jesus. I stand firm in my position as an adopted child of God. I reject the lies Satan tells me that I am unworthy or not good enough. I rejoice in the truth that Jesus is always for me and loves me just as I am.

121

Your Creator Answers

God will design help to meet
your unique, individual, and specific needs.

*I look up to the mountains and hills, longing for God's help. But
then I realize that our true help and protection come only from
the Lord, our Creator who made the heavens and the earth*
(Psalm 121:1-2).

Where can you find help when you really need it? This writer
started first by looking to nature, the beauty that surrounded him,
but he came up empty. Help won't come from a high hill, from a
bank account, or a job.

It's great to be able to turn to loved ones, family members,
friends, or other supporters—they will be able to help some of the
time, but some things will be beyond them. We all learn, as this
writer did, that only our Lord and King Jesus can protect us from
the really big things that come our way.

This psalm goes on to say that the Lord will not let your foot
to be moved and that the Lord will guard you and keep you. You
can count on him at any time—he is never sleeping when you call
out to him; his eyes never leave you. He is uniquely qualified to be
your help. He made you and understands your unique make-up,
your strengths, and weaknesses. And he sees ahead to the best path
for your life.

━━━◆◆◆━━━

I love the beautiful pictures of God's creation—a majestic
mountain or a beautiful lake. But when I need help, I look to the
Creator, not the creation, for answers, encouragement, rescue, and
hope. I can count on him fashioning his help uniquely for me.

122

A Prosperous Life

Soak deep in Jesus, experience his peace, security and joy in your soul.

O Jerusalem, may there be peace for those who dwell inside your walls and prosperity in your every palace (Psalm 122:7).

The new Jerusalem is made up of us—a family of people who are followers of Jesus. The promises made about Jerusalem apply to you as a member of God's adopted family.

God's desire is for you to live in peace and for your life to prosper and be secure. While you might think first of your physical world, this applies even more so to your spiritual life. There is no guarantee that your body might not be destroyed by accident or disease, but there is a guarantee that your spirit will thrive. When your spirit is secure and your soul under the care of Jesus, you can live in peace.

And because of Jesus, you are assured that your soul will flourish during your time on earth. You can live every day with a trustworthy belief that God will make your soul prosper and that you will live a life that counts for Jesus and is full of joy, hope, and contentment.

Peace, security, and prosperity are yours to experience each day you draw breath. And they change everything. They move us from a drab life to one that makes you glad to awake each morning. Seek them, grab them, and make them your experience.

———

By letting Jesus into every corner of my life, I get to experience what everyone in the world wants—peace, security, and a soul that prospers every day. And I have the power I need in Jesus to choose to be happy.

123

On Jesus' Lap

**Sit quietly with Jesus, look into his eyes;
mercy and love will abound for you.**

The way I love you is like the way a servant wants to please his master, the way a maid waits for the orders of her mistress. We look to you, our God, with passionate longing to please you and discover more of your mercy and grace (Psalm 123:2).

A servant in those days had nothing without their master. Spiritually, you are like that today. Without your master (Jesus), you wouldn't have any of his gifts like love, joy, peace, patience, and so on that make life fun and enjoyable. Like non-believers, you might have brief periods of these, but you wouldn't be surrounded by them like you are now.

Listen to your own experiences that tell you that you cannot take care of yourself. Open yourself up to the idea that surrendering your all to Jesus puts you on the path of his gifts. In this way, be a servant to your King. The more you surrender, the more freedom you will have.

Earthly masters (like bosses or politicians) will disappoint you. Keeping your eyes and thoughts on Jesus will help you walk in joy and obedience to his directions. And make you happier. You can feed the fire of your own joy by desiring to please God with all your emotions. Everyone who gives the Lord their heart is rewarded with peace.

I want to spend more time with Jesus every day. I want my turning to him become more and more automatic. I want to engage all my emotions when I sit quietly with him, or when I talk to him or worship him. My sweet Jesus, how I love you!

124

Live Confidently

**Jesus breaks down the plans that are against you.
He lives for your freedom.**

We are free from the hunter's trap; their snare is broken, and we have escaped! (Psalm 124:7)

The Lord has given us many promises. You know that his steadfast love and faithfulness always cover you, that he is full of mercy, and that he has a formed a plan to give you a great future and hope. You can count on each of these promises.

But you also know that you still face dangers in the world. God's Word tells you that Satan, your great enemy, is actively looking for ways to destroy you. This verse shows a different danger—a cleverly laid trap, placed to ensnare the unwary. But no matter if the attack is loud and scary or quiet and hidden, the Lord has given you a way of victory over any method by which you might be targeted.

When you are walking with the Lord, he sees the trap and breaks its power to let you escape. He doesn't always destroy the trap before you step in it. Sometimes he lets you learn from your escape. But in all cases, he has you covered—from a lion-like frontal attack to a quiet snare that would deny your freedom. None of these will flourish against you.

———

Thank you, Jesus, for my many rescues. Sometimes you have directed me away from the attack, and sometimes you have rescued me out of the snare I was foolish enough to step into. I love your protection and your rescue. Keep me on your path, which is safe and filled with goodness.

125

Active Trust

Renew your faith and hope-filled expectation in Jesus every day. He will make you strong.

Those who trust in the Lord are as unshakable, as unmovable as the mighty Mount Zion! (Psalm 125:1)

This is a great promise—that you, as a Jesus follower, are as incapable of being moved as a huge mountain! At first you might think—wait, that can't be true—I follow Jesus, but I have been shaken and moved. You've gone off course, as have all believers.

So then, what does this mean? Trust is the key. Trust here is not a casual thing. It is a minute-by-minute total reliance on Jesus. It is putting your own resources on the back burner and placing all you have on the Lord. When you trust that way, your faith is made strong, and you become unshakable.

Physically you might tremble, but spiritually you will be strong. You will be able to use your faith to resist Satan and his attacks. You will be able to renounce him and order him to leave you, using the blood of Jesus to drive him away.

Make your trust active. Yesterday's trust won't be enough to rescue you today. Your faith needs to be on-going, renewed, and strengthened every day. Temptations and fears will come your way, but they won't have the power to overcome you; you will defeat them.

———

Temptations and fears that come against me are powerless in the face of my faith and trust in Jesus. That sounds audacious, but it is the full truth. I will call on the Holy Spirit to fill me each day, and he will make me solid. Jesus is more than a match for the schemes of my enemy.

126

Overcoming Heartache

**Tears will come but keep investing
your life in Jesus by helping others.**

*They may weep as they go out carrying their seed to sow, but
they will return with joyful laughter and shouting with gladness as they bring back armloads of blessing and a harvest overflowing!* (Psalm 126:6)

This is a beautiful picture of a way to handle heartbreak—by
investing your life into the lives of others, both believers and those
not yet redeemed. Like these people, don't sit at home and wonder
if God has left you—go out and create a new tomorrow for you
and others.

God honors that kind of response from you. Instead of getting
stuck in fear or even sadness, you will be blessed when you keep on
sowing. Keep on investing your faith into your life and the lives of
others, and you will also be fed by this crop. This takes faith, believing you will receive what you can't see, but look at the rewards
of being obedient to God's call.

Your faith-work might be done in sorrow or pain, but it will
yield great harvests. You will see people being blessed, being set
free, being lifted from sorrow to joy. You will be helping people;
you will give them courage to keep trying. When you see those
things, you will be filled with exuberant joy that will overcome your
own tears. Imagine on your own what armloads of blessings in your
life will look like.

I will face times of sorrow and grief. It probably won't be easy,
but I will keep trusting in Jesus and keep helping other people. I
will be able to laugh with joy, and I will be blessed to overflowing.

127

Your Work Made Rich

**Be humble before the Lord;
he will make your work worthwhile.**

*If God's grace doesn't help the builders, they will labor in vain
to build a house. If God's mercy doesn't protect the city, all the
sentries will circle it in vain* (Psalm 127:1).

Most all of us have a job that we work at for years at a time.
Sometimes we like the job, sometimes not. This verse speaks to
this toil and says that when you invite the Lord into your work and
give your job to the Lord, your efforts will be enriched and more
successful.

It's a great relief to know that you are not solely responsible for
the results of your work. The Lord wants you to do your work
heartily and to invite his active involvement in your job. When you
do, your work will not be done in vain—the hours you invest each
day will result in a rich reward for you and others.

Ask the Holy Spirit to enrich the work you do by giving you
all you need for your job each day. Putting your reliance on God's
grace and mercy at your work will give you confidence—his desires
for you are way better than any you can dream up. That gives you
freedom and even joy to seek his direction in everything you do for
your work.

———

There is tremendous freedom in giving Jesus control over my
work efforts. I want my work and everything I do to make an impact on the people around me. I continually rely on God's grace
and mercy to tenderize my heart and see the needs around me.

128

A Goodness-Fest

God will bless your work when you
honor him and walk with him.

Your reward will be prosperity, happiness, and well-being (Psalm 128:2).

This verse, along with verse one, are a gigantic goodness-fest! Look at the over-the-top fantastic gifts God promises to those who are humble before him and obey. First, you will be joyous. That's a huge thing, especially in a world that throws a lot more bad news at you than good. Joyous—as in deep, ongoing and satisfying delight. Your mind, your decision making, your emotions will all be firing from a foundation of gladness and peace.

And added to that are prosperity, happiness, and your well-being, all these being given freely and generously to those who obey God. Obeying the Lord is rewarding all on its own; the bonuses of joy and well-being shows how greatly you are favored by your King. Think of waking each day to an amazing confidence because of how the Lord has blessed you.

Fellow follower of Jesus, open your heart and put him first in your life, making him your king. You'll have fewer times when you can't make up your mind what is the right thing to do. You will get more and more used to hearing God speak to you. Your love for worship will grow, as will your love for the people around you.

I am flat out amazed by my Savior Jesus. His desire to make my life bountiful is more than I can ever have hoped or imagined. I bow my head to him, and I want to obey his every wish. I thank him for his lavish bounty to my life.

129

God Covets Your Freedom

**God loves freedom. He will set you free—
call on him and live close to him.**

*But no matter what, the Lord is good to us. He is a righteous
God who stood to defend us, breaking the chains of the evil ones
that bound us* (Psalm 129:4).

When something bad happens to you, remember the Lord
proved that he loves you when Jesus went to the cross to die for
you and your sins. Fall back on that truth when you face the unknown or sadness. Take a deep breath and thank him for his great
love, even in the midst of sorrow.

Those who are against you, whether human or spiritual, will
not win the battles they bring against you. You will be victorious
against spiritual attacks that try to defeat you. Sometimes they gain
ground, and you may end up in some type of captivity that keeps
you from living the free life God has for you.

But take courage from the promises in this verse. Jesus is your
righteousness, and he will break any chains that weigh you down
and try to rob you of your freedom. Jesus will always be your defender and treat you tenderly. Remember, he wants your freedom
even more than you do.

Jesus has shattered chains I have faced. Together with him, I
have the authority to win and always be the victor. He has also
used worship, prayer, and his written words to set me free. I will
maximize my freedom by walking close to Jesus.

130

No Shortages

Forgiveness creates freedom.

O Israel, keep hoping, keep trusting, and keep waiting on the Lord, for he is tenderhearted, kind, and forgiving. He has a thousand ways to set you free! (Psalm 130:7)

What does God's steadfast hope and trust look like in your life? Think of having your emotions and your mind comforted in the face of a deep loss. Be assured of being faithfully guided through making the hardest decisions you will ever face. God's steadfast love is far above your love. You will never face a shortage of God's love; it never dims.

The picture of God's tenderhearted forgiveness to you is amazing. Your redemption on the cross is beyond measure—your redemption is full and robust. It is all you will ever need, covering your sins in the past and in the future.

And isn't it fun to see that Jesus has thousands of way to set you free! His forgiveness is very rich, and it also leads to the Lord continually releasing you from captivity and finding unique ways to do so. Be encouraged—Jesus is always renewing and refreshing your life to bring you to new levels of freedom.

———◆———

I claim in full confidence that I am totally redeemed and that the Lord sees me as holy. And I also claim that each day he is making me more holy. He brings my soul to life, and my heart rests in his beauty for me.

131

Peace in His Eyes

**You can have perfect peace.
Give yourself fully to Jesus, rest in his arms.**

I am humbled and quieted in your presence. Like a contented child who rests on its mother's lap, I'm your resting child and my soul is content in you (Psalm 131:2).

Picture your child, or someone you know, resting in Mom's arms. That is the very picture of peace and quiet. Jesus wants to bring this to your soul (your mind, your will, and your emotions). To get quiet, take your focus off yourself and put it on Jesus. Leave behind all that is going on in the moment or the day and think, feel, desire only Jesus.

In that place you will find yourself free from anxiety or concern—just like a child does when being comforted by their mother. You will hold no grudges or complaints. Your total focus on Jesus means you don't have to worry about what is going to happen next. Your contentment in the moment will fill you up.

Be like a child; it's natural and right to be in Jesus' arms. It's peaceful even though the moments leading up to it might have been hectic. Your whole body will relax, as will your mind, when you melt into Jesus' lap. Your eyes will be calm, and your breathing will be peaceful. That's the picture of resting in Jesus.

I've seen this picture with my kids and now grandchildren—it is beautiful. Jesus wants to give this same thing to me. To rest in Jesus isn't to empty my mind, it is to focus my mind, my will, and my emotions on Jesus—to let him control them. I know the Prince of Peace will bring me peace

132

At His Feet

**You can worship God wherever you are.
Give it a try; you will be blessed.**

*Let's go into God's dwelling place and bow down and worship
before him* (Psalm 132:7).

Place was very important to people living when this was
written. Today, instead of place, our focus is on the person of Jesus.
We worship God wherever we are. You can find God in the gro-
cery store, at work, at your kitchen table, or in your church
building. Any place where you bow before the Lord and worship
him becomes a sacred place.

That means that you can be drawn closer to God wherever you
are. You can focus on the person of awe—Jesus. Your songs of worship might be in your heart, instead of out loud like they are in
church, but they are equally as meaningful to your soul.

And there are some things of worship that are better done outside the church building—like praying for a sick person in their
home or telling a stranger about Jesus and the peace he can bring
to them and their household. Both these are acts of worship just
like singing a song during a worship service.

Form a habit of praising God in your soul all the time.
Recognize that the greatest "place" of worship is a footstool before
Jesus.

⫸•⫷

I am learning to do this, and I find I have to be very purposeful, or I forget and my mind wanders. When I do focus on
Jesus, I find blessings all the time. I don't get upset about delays. I
see needs that I didn't used to see. My heart is peaceful, knowing
that Jesus is always beside me.

133

Honor Your Friends

Seek peace with others; make them more important; pray for them.

How truly wonderful and delightful it is to see brothers and sisters living together in sweet unity! (Psalm 133:1)

The image that comes to mind is of a family or a group of friends living in peace, happiness, and contentment. They are drawn together for a common purpose—to bring life to their family members and their friends. There may be disagreements, but there is no strife because everyone is learning to give grace and mercy and to grant and seek forgiveness.

How can you grow this type of atmosphere? The foundation is the bond of Jesus holding your friends together. Even among those who are not followers of Jesus, honor them by loving them, praying for and with them, and extending peace and love to them. Demonstrate your love by what you say and what you do. Ask God to magnify your love to them.

Show each person they are loved and accepted. Learn to give some leeway to others. Make the bridge you are walking on together as wide as you can.

Decide that you are all going to be great together. Seek each other out, be honest with each other and also full of grace. Sacrifice what you want for the sake of another person—count others as more important than you are.

———

I want my groups to be like this. I will pray through the ups and downs of my family and friend groups. I will accept all of them through disappointments and hurts that we all feel. I will seek ways to help them, as I know they will for me.

134

Love Notes

**God desires your praise; he knows it will
make you happier and improve your life.**

*...lifting up your hands in holy worship; come and bless the
Lord!* (Psalm 134:2)

Think of when you received a nice note or email from a friend
or one of your children, and how encouraged you felt. In a similar
way, you can be blessed by the Lord when you worship him, ex-
pressly by lifting up your hands in holy worship. He will send a
love note to your heart!

Do you ever wonder how the Lord feels when you lift your
hands up to him? The Father expressed emotions, as did Jesus.
From his anger at sin to his compassion for you, God is moved by
things happening to you. Your worship also moves him; his unmeasurable peace and joy are released by your praise.

A big part of why the Lord asks for your praise is because he
knows that your worship will help you love him more, which will
lead to a happier life for you. Your praise doesn't increase his love
for you—he can't love you any more than he already does. But it
will open you up to more of his blessings. You will become more
aware of the great gifts he wants to give you.

It is exciting for me to know that my King desires my praise,
not because he needs it or has an ego to feed, but because he knows
the act of praising him will increase my joy. I know that the Lord
of the universe is vitally interested in me, and worshipping Jesus is
one of the ways he will create a more abundant life for me.

135

Bringing Greatness

**The Lord is filled with power and good;
there is no hint of any wrong or bad in him.**

*He does what he pleases, with unlimited power and authority,
extending his greatness throughout the entire universe!* (Psalm
135:6)

Earlier in this chapter, the Lord is described as being good.
This is different than a person who is described as good—because
no matter how good that person acts, you know that good people
can also be selfish and fearful. But that's not so with the Lord,
whose acts are good because the entirety of his being is good.
There is not even a hint of anything less than pure in him.

When God acts with power and authority, you can be comforted by knowing those actions are for your good. His power is
equally mixed with his love, and his actions come from pure compassion and peace. Plenty of bad things may come your way, but
you can be sure that none of them come from God. He proved he
is worthy of your trust because of what he did for you at Calvary.

His perfect mix of power and goodness means you can sit
comfortably with Jesus. You can always approach him in peace. He
is pleased with you; you are his beloved son or daughter. He desires
your companionship and will bring greatness to your life.

———◆———

Jesus' name is beautiful, and I trust him and all his power to
bring beauty into my life. I will never have anything to fear in
talking with God—his mercy and grace are always pouring over
me. Wherever I go, his power goes before me, and I will wash in
his goodness and beauty.

136

Priceless, Tender Love

God adopted you when you had nothing to offer; always be thankful to him.

He's the God who chose us when we were nothing! His tender love for us continues on forever! (Psalm 136:23)

One of the reasons why it's easy to believe in the greatness of God is that he knows we are not like him. Jesus is mighty, having formed the earth so we could enjoy living on it. He helps you defeat enemies who want to steal your joy. Yet he never forgets that on your own, you are not full of great power or influence.

Best of all, he continues to pour out his love over you and over each new generation born on earth. Every day, every hour, every minute, his steadfast love covers you and nurtures you. He re-forms your character and re-news your life every day. He empowers you to live in ways you can't even imagine could be true.

The picture of his tender love is priceless. Compare this to a mom with a new baby—few things are more tender than that, but Jesus' love for you surpasses that. Sometimes you can't see that love clearly, so you will need to believe in that love by faith. Prepare your faith by treasuring what he has done for you and thanking him every day.

————

I smile big when I imagine God looking at me. I had nothing to offer him except my brokenness, and that was good with him. He chose me when I had nothing and gave me eternal life and the Holy Spirit so I could live with him. There are times when I continue to offer him very little, and in response, he continues to freely give me his tender love.

137

Toughen Up Your Faith

**Faith will be hard sometimes—hang onto it,
never give it up. It will rescue you.**

*Our music and mirth were no longer heard, only sadness. We
hung up our harps on the willow trees* (Psalm 137:2).

This is a tough, emotional chapter. It shows the natural reaction people have to harsh and brutal treatment and to captivity. The writer has been made a prisoner and has been tormented by his captors who have also destroyed his home city of Jerusalem. Horrible things had been done to them and the people they loved. Thus, they had stopped singing and worshipping. We might react the same way.

They had given up hope of ever getting out of their situation. They could not envision their city being restored. But even so, they vowed to never forget their place of worship—which to them meant never forgetting their God. They had succumbed to the torture and the mocking, but they hung onto a remnant of their faith.

You should pay attention to this history. Similar things could happen to you, spiritually if not physically. Satan's task is to take away your freedom and destroy your hope. Never stop fighting your enemy; those are battles you will win. Keep calling on Jesus to rescue you—don't give up. Keep declaring your hope and freedom. Jesus has given you authority to be the winner. Draw ever closer to him, especially as you see danger coming.

I will not let Satan have my future, my hope or my freedom. I will constantly humble myself before Jesus and call on his power to defeat any plans Satan has for me. I declare they will amount to nothing. In that way, I will always live in hope.

138

Lots of Listen

The Lord will quickly rejuvenate your soul when you call on him.

At the very moment I called out to you, you answered me! You strengthened me deep within my soul and breathed fresh courage into me (Psalm 138:3).

Does it seem like it takes a long time for some prayers to be answered? This is especially true when the prayer is about some physical circumstance—a job, health, or finances. We all ache to see God's answers in those areas.

This verse challenges the notion that God's answers are late. It says that God answered right away and that the answer gave strength and courage to the one who was praying. God hears every prayer, but his timing is beyond any of us to explain.

It seems that prayers in the spiritual realm are answered quickly. God acts in your soul right away, for example, clearing your mind to give direction in the face of many choices, giving your will the courage to make a decision, or freeing your emotions from fear over a decision. Your soul can be changed in a moment.

So can your physical world, but the timing to those answers seems more uncertain. And sometimes the answer to your prayer is no. There is often tension between what you want and what the Lord knows is best for you. You will need to live by faith in that tension—believing that God loves you and will only give you good things.

I will trust the Lord with all my requests about my physical world, knowing that my vision in those areas is very limited or self-seeking. I choose to believe he will bring me goodness, even if I must wait. I rely with certainty for him to rejuvenate my soul.

139

Always Choose Love

**Jesus surrounds your past and your future.
He is always bringing good into your life.**

You've gone into my future to prepare the way, and in kindness you follow behind me to spare me from the harm of my past. With our hand of love on my life, you impart a blessing to me (Psalm 139:5).

The Lord's grace and mercy are overwhelming. He always chooses love and treats you with unwavering compassion. No matter what path you have travelled, Jesus' love and kindness covers your life. You can't earn it, but you can be sure that he wipes away your past and prepares you for your future because his everlasting choice is to pour out his love on you.

God will help you and others heal from the harm of your past. He will help you seek forgiveness from those you have harmed and will erase the stain of your sin from your conscience (Psalm 51:2). Trust that he is always going into your unknown future to make it into the best for you. All his actions are bringing good to you and demonstrating his love for you.

The Lord's presence will encourage you to choose the right paths—and it won't be burdensome to do so. You will experience increasing gladness as you choose to follow his will. You will see that choosing what God wants never means you are missing out—instead, it always means you are getting more.

I can trust God with my future—his kindness is always looking out for me and will always bring goodness into my life. I thank Jesus for wiping away my sin and helping remove and heal the damage my sins have caused me and others. I live in gratitude to my King.

140

Be Prepared for Evil

God has given you authority and powerful weapons to use over your spiritual enemies.

He concocts his secret strategy to divide and harm others, stirring up trouble one against another (Psalm 140:2).

The "he" here is Satan and evil men controlled by him. They were out to destroy David. They wanted to bring ruin to David's life. That's been Satan's goal since he rebelled against the Lord. His strategies are to work in secret, to divide followers of Jesus, and to create tension so that people fall into dissension and distrust with others.

It's good to know your enemy. It's even better to know, and to claim out loud, that he is already defeated. You are assured of victory because Jesus defeated Satan and death when he died on the cross and then was raised from the dead. Don't be discouraged that you have an enemy. Rejoice that he has been defeated and that you can bring him and his strategies to complete and utter ruin!

Be aware that evil exists for the purpose of ruining the lives of Jesus' believers. Know that you have the authority and power of Jesus' name and shed blood to stand up to Satan and evil. Use spiritual weapons in your battles, such as forgiveness, God's written Word, worship, your own prayer and the prayers of other believers, and your total dependence on God's love.

------◆◆◆------

I won't let spiritual enemies sneak up on me. I know they want to separate me from other believers—I won't let that happen. I will ask for forgiveness and forgive. I will learn how to use my authority in Jesus to confront my spiritual enemies.

141

A Strong Defense

**Hide yourself in Jesus every day,
look into his eyes and worship him.**

*But you are my Lord and my God; I have eyes only for you! I
hide myself in you, so don't leave me defenseless* (Psalm 141:8).

This was written by King David. He had guards all around
him, but he knew his protection really came from the Lord. David
was very humble. He put himself under the authority of the Lord
and said that his best hiding place was God, on whom he counted
for defense.

Like David, be humble and acknowledge that you are under
God's leadership and the Lord is the final ruler in your life. That is
a choice that takes wisdom and trust. It's so easy to think that you
can handle your life yourself. That's a trap, and one that is likely to
bring you a hectic pace you can't meet and heartache, not comfort.

Learn to focus your attention on Jesus. You shortchange yourself when you focus too much on your own problems, your next
quarter, or your next deal. There is so much more joy in placing
your hope in Jesus and letting him deal with what's next in your
life. Call on Jesus to be your defender. Be upfront about your needs
and concerns. Jesus is eager to meet your needs and calm your
fears, so open yourself to him and receive what he has for you.

I need my time with Jesus to visualize him leading my day. I
need my eyes focused on him. I will call on Jesus to be my King
every day and ask the Holy Spirit to fill me with the wisdom and
joy I need for each day.

142

No Dungeon for You

**Praise Jesus for your freedom.
Enjoy it with your great friends.**

*Bring me out of this dungeon so I can declare your praise! And
all your godly lovers will celebrate all the wonderful things
you've done for me!* (Psalm 142:7)

David's dungeon was the cave he was hiding in. People wanted
to kill him, but he knew he was innocent of the reasons they
wanted him dead. We all have our own caves or prisons—some we
cause by our own behaviors, and some we are unjustly put in by our
enemies.

Many verses in the Psalms deal with your spiritual freedom.
The Lord knows that this is a real issue for many of his children.
Perhaps you have been a spiritual prisoner or captive at some time
in your life, or maybe you are now. If so, cry out to the Lord for
your freedom. Reject Satan and all his ways, surrender yourself
completely to the Lord, and ask the Holy Spirit to fill your life
with his goodness.

These steps, along with your obedience to Jesus, will lead to
your freedom. Then use your freedom to engage in a life of helping
other people—that will also help you stay free. And make friends
with people who are also walking with Jesus. Stand by them, and
ask them to stand by you. Invest in those friendships. Celebrate
God's goodness with them.

I will never let myself be a prisoner or captive. Jesus said he
came to set me free, and free is what I will be! I will draw near to
Jesus, and he will draw near to me. I will count on my friends to
help me when I'm down and bring joy to my life.

143

Today Is Brand New

God will reveal his warm, kind and strong love to you every day.

Let the dawning day bring me revelation of your tender, unfailing love. Give me light for my path and teach me, for I trust in you (Psalm 143:8).

There are days when you need so much to know God's deep care over your life. What you are facing may be life threatening. Or it may be an ongoing battle with something that is dragging you down little by little. You need to regain your sense of who you are (the righteousness of Jesus) and whose you are (you belong to Jesus who bought your redemption at a great price).

It is enriching to know that you can wake up every day with fresh insight into the Lord's love and a renewed mind, covered with mercies designed just for what you need today. It is so powerful and comforting to know that his tender love is mightier than the strongest wall you face. Jesus' love for you never wavers, not even one tiny little bit.

Jesus is your stronghold. Let that lift your soul. Today is brand new in God's economy. Lay aside whatever junk you faced yesterday. Make time to let Jesus talk with you today. He wants to reveal new discoveries of his love and show you a great way forward from where you are.

Jesus, thank you for giving me fresh guidance for today. I revel in your new mercies and your tender yet powerful love. I am glad to put my trust in you—help me to trust you even more tomorrow. Thank you for the joy and contentment you give to me.

144

Prayers for Your Children

Pray continually that your children will make Jesus their Lord.

Deliver us! Then our homes will be happy. Our sons will grow up as strong, sturdy men and our daughters with graceful beauty, royally fashioned as for a palace (Psalm 144:12).

This psalm was written as David prepared for his battle with Goliath. He wanted assurance that the sons of his people would be strong, full of the fruit of their lives, and that their daughters would demonstrate graceful beauty and be strong enough to be like pillars for a palace. For himself, David knew that physical strength would not win his battle; he would rely on the Lord, not his sword or spear.

Strong men and women, who are willing to put down deep roots in Jesus, are needed today more than ever. They will be strong support structures for their families and be filled with grace.

How can you help create people who will take on the toils of adulthood and create positive families and cultures? This chapter says to encourage your children to make the Lord their rock and refuge, to be willing to be trained by the Lord, to choose to live by faith when doubt is so easy, and to stay away from those who lie. As a family, worship the Lord and be happy when God is your Lord.

———

It makes me glad when I see these traits demonstrated in my adult children. I know the Lord has blessed them and me through them. I will continue to pray for my children and for theirs. The Lord will honor those prayers for generations.

145

Your Heart's Longings

**God will richly bless your love for him;
he understands your heart and will provide.**

*Every one of your godly lovers receives even more than what
they ask for. For you hear what their hearts really long for and
you bring them your saving strength* (Psalm 145:19).

What does your heart long for? It's exciting that the Lord
knows exactly what it is—even if you have trouble describing it.
And what's the word that describes how you feel when you realize
that God is committed to bringing you the desires of your heart?
What's the word that describes your feelings when you get more
than you asked for? Sometimes it seems like there are no words
good enough!

This verse also says the Lord will bring you saving strength,
which is really the foundation for who you want be for the rest of
your life. Your life is redeemed, and your sins have been washed
away. Be assured that your soul is being renewed every day, and
someday you will get a whole new body through which you will
worship the Lord and have enjoyment forever.

Those thoughts will invigorate you. Maybe they describe what
you really want more than anything. You can live without guilt and
shame and rest in glorious peace and contentment. You can live beyond what you could ever have hoped for—that's being rich!

———◆———

Jesus created a world filled with kindness. But sin created great
havoc, and we can all see the results in our world. This verse reas-
sures me that I don't need to be bogged down in the mess of this
world. I claim the Holy Spirit's gifts of love, joy, peace, goodness,
and others for me. They are mine right now.

146

Hope Generates Happiness

**God will renew your hope.
His "sure thing" hope will bring you joy.**

But those who hope in the Lord will be happy and pleased. Our help comes from the God of Jacob! (Psalm 146:5)

There is beauty in this verse as it calls the Lord both your hope and your help. If you were not sure that God was able to provide help when you needed it, you'd have little reason for hope. And if you didn't place your hope in the Lord, you wouldn't ask for his help.

In this way hope and help are entwined together. At the core, hope in the Lord is based on his redemption of your life. Jesus understands that hope feeds on help actually being delivered. Don't hesitate to go to the Lord for help; and when he delivers, make note of it so you don't forget. Times of answered help will heap up and give you more reason for hope.

Hope generates happiness and pleasure. God so wants you to be happy in your life. Take advantage of God's cycle of goodness—when you are empty, cry out to the Lord for help. He knows what you need and will start refreshing your mind and delivering help. This will grow your confidence in Jesus, which will cause you to hope even more and lead to greater joy in your life.

———◆———

My hope sometimes starts out as a trickle, maybe even more of a wish. It grows as I learn and see that Jesus is my great and trustworthy help. This turns my trickle of wishes and hopes into a stream of living hope that generates joy in my heart.

147

Make Beauty Happen

Worship creates beauty, delights the Lord, and makes you dazzling in his eyes.

Hallelujah! Praise the Lord! How beautiful it is when we sing our praises to the beautiful God, for praise makes you lovely before him and brings him great delight! (Psalm 147:1)

We all want more beauty in our lives. We seek grace, tenderness, and hopefulness in people we like to be around. And we look for loveliness in nature. Who wouldn't rather look at a beautiful lake surrounded by trees than gaze at a dirty alleyway somewhere. We are drawn to beauty because we have been made by a God whose character is beauty.

Many ugly things happen in life. How much better off you are when you focus on beauty. Here's an amazing truth for you—you can not only focus your mind and eyes on things of beauty, you can actually help create them!

Singing and worshipping the Lord make beauty happen. And another amazing thing—your praise helps make you lovely before the Lord. Jesus always looks at you with favor, this is even grander—your praises make you lovely to him.

And there is still more. Your praise brings God great delight—not just a little happiness but great delight. And that delight reflects on you, bringing more and more happiness to your soul. This is another cycle of goodness that Jesus brings to you. So, sing and praise him when you need a little delight.

This verse amazes me. How often I settle for just getting by, when I could be creating beauty, giving God delight, and having that delight settle back on me. That moves my heart and stirs up my soul.

148

Amazed by His Goodness

The Lord will flood your life with strength, esteem, and respect.

He anoints his people with strength and authority, showing his great favor to all his godly lovers, even to his princely people, Israel, who are so close to his heart. Hallelujah! Praise the Lord! (Psalm 148:14)

You are "his people." The King of the universe pours out strength and authority on you and all who love the Lord. You are a powerful person in God's spiritual realm. You have been given authority over your spiritual enemies—you are above them and, in the name of Jesus, you can command them. Use your strength in Jesus to chase away anything that wants to steal from your life.

The Lord knows what you face each day. He knows that sometimes sin and going in the wrong direction are right outside your door. That's why he has gifted you with the Holy Spirit and the wisdom to turn away from sin. You can be the person you have always wanted to be, but somehow could never quite get there, when you walk in his freedom.

He has done this because you are so close to his heart. This love causes him to shower you with favor—to put you in good situations where you can prosper and be happy. When you are facing trouble, are tempted, or are just poor in spirit, remember that the King is always raining strength, authority, and favor over your life.

I am amazed at the goodness of my Lord. I sit back and relax in his care over me. He counts me as one of his princely people, and he holds me close to his heart. He gives me the power to live a lovely life.

149

Crazy in Love

Jesus loves to be around you;
he brings beauty to your inner being.

For he enjoys his faithful lovers. He adorns the humble with his beauty and he loves to give them the victory (Psalm 149:4).

The greatest thing is to know your King and Savior takes pleasure in you and loves to be with you. This is so good that it's sometimes hard to accept because, like all believers, you know how far short you have come sometimes. But it is an absolute truth—Jesus loves to be around you. He is crazy in love with you. He gets a kick out of you.

You are the only one that can interrupt your sense of that. It's sad, but you can turn away and put up a roadblock between you and Jesus, short-circuiting your ability to see clearly his love for you. But nothing stops the abiding love he has for you. So, don't go there. Instead, live a life of obedience and repentance.

It's maybe a little odd to put those two words in the same sentence. After all, if we are obedient, why do we need repentance? Because God knows you won't always be obedient. He loves for you to enjoy a close relationship with him. So, when you do sin, quickly and humbly repent, and you'll again see his stream of gifts renew your life.

———◆———

God is happy with me—I will live in that truth. My praise lifts his heart and brings joy to mine. He loves nothing more than to give me victory in my life. He is for me and is always on my side. He adorns me with beauty in my soul.

150

Learn to Love Worshiping

Give your all to Jesus; he will do mighty things in your life.

Praise him for his miracles of might! Praise him for his magnif-icent greatness! (Psalm 150:2)

You have seen how the Psalms are full of ups and downs. David and the other writers are full of anguish and overcome with joy. But more than anything you have seen lots of praise and worship of the King of kings. One big take-away from the Psalms is that God adores your worship, and he always pours out his blessings on those who worship him.

Learn to love to worship by worshipping with your whole heart. If you tend to be more subdued, that's okay. But give yourself permission to stretch a bit at times. Go overboard in expressing your admiration for his beauty, his tenderness, and his care. While you are saying these words, ask God to tell you how he feels about you as you sing them. This could open a big, wonderful world to you.

You have also seen that God is full of faithfulness and steadfast love. Imitate him. Choose to love in all circumstances, even and especially when it means you are sacrificing something to do so. Practice praise and thankfulness. Walk in the joy of the Lord and you will walk with favor and authority. You will live in ever-growing joy and contentment. And you will be surrounded by people who love you.

I am so blessed. Out of a mess God has created a person who loves, who revels in praising God, who hears from him regularly, and who lives in favor and freedom. I am loved by God and my family; I lack nothing. I praise the Lord for these great gifts.